How to Turn Trends Into Fortunes

How to Turn Trends Into Fortunes Without Getting Left in the Dust

STU TAYLOR

WITH TOM BIRACREE

A Birch Lane Press Book

Published by Carol Publishing Group

A Birch Lane Press Book
Published by Carol Publishing Group
Birch Lane Press is a registered trademark of Carol Communications, Inc.
Editorial Offices: 600 Madison Avenue, New York, N.Y. 10022
Sales and Distribution Offices: 120 Enterprise Avenue, Secaucus, N.J. 07094
In Canada: Canadian Manda Group, P.O. Box 920, Station U, Toronto, Ontario M8Z 5P9
Queries regarding rights and permissions should be addressed to Carol Publishing Group, 600 Madison Avenue, New York, N.Y. 10022

Carol Publishing Group books are available at special discounts for bulk purchases, for sales promotions, fund raising, or educational purposes. Special editions can be created to specifications. For details, contact Special Sales Department, Carol Publishing Group, 120 Enterprise Avenue, Secaucus, N.J. 07094

Manufactured in the United States of America
10 9 8 7 6 5 4 3 2 1

Library of Congress Cataloging-in-Publication Data
Taylor, Stu.
  How to turn trends into fortunes without getting left in the dust / by Stu Taylor with Tom Biracree.
      p.   cm.
  "A Birch Lane Press book."
  ISBN 1-55972-171-5
  1. New products—United States—Marketing.   2. Fads—United States—Marketing.   I. Biracree, Tom, 1947-   . II. Title.
HF5415.153.T4   1993
658.5'75—dc20   92-39830
                                                   CIP

Dedicated

to my wife, Diane,
and daughters, Andrea and Carla;

to my brother, Jason, and his wife, Gail;

and in loving memory of my parents, Bert and Esther.

Acknowledgments

Many thanks to my wife, Diane, who continually supports me in all of my endeavors, has given me so much practical advice in the writing of this book, and is the key person in my life as well as in my business.

I'm grateful to my brother, Jason, who spent many hours assisting me with this book as he has countless other times during my life, and his wife, Gail, whose efforts resulted in many typed manuscript pages.

My gratitude to my dear friend, Anthony Summers, who is always available with his support and sound advice, and to Cecile Fraser of Taylor Associates, Inc., who lives daily with all of my business ventures and *How to Turn Trends Into Fortunes*.

Many thanks to Tony Seidl and Dave Weiner, without whom this book would not have been published by the Carol Publishing Group, and to Tom Biracree, who so eloquently captured the essence of my thoughts and worked with me to transcribe them into text.

My appreciation to the entire Carol Publishing Group, headed by Steven Schragis, whose belief in my project will always have special meaning to me, to Bruce Shostak, who showed so much patience and consideration in editing this book, and to Deborah Feingertz and Gary Fitzgerald.

I'm indebted to Jim Sullivan of the *Boston Globe* and to David Alpern and Bill Barol of *Newsweek*, who afforded me the opportunity to address a national audience.

Contents

Introduction

Men are born to succeed, not to fail.
　　　　—Henry David Thoreau

If you take just one kernel of wisdom from reading these pages, it should be this: The gloomy economic headlines that have dominated the business pages for the last couple of years should fill you with hope, not despair. For people with initiative, courage, and desire, this decade will bring unprecedented prosperity. If you're skeptical, don't just listen to Stu Taylor, listen to *USA Today*:

> The 1990s will present more exciting and more lucrative opportunities to Americans with the entrepreneurial spirit than any other time in our history.

Having the entrepreneurial spirit means that you and I understand that our economic fortunes don't depend on whatever Bill Clinton, Alan Greenspan, the U.S. Congress, Saddam Hussein, or our bosses decide to do or not do. Let the economic pundits and politicians fret about stagnant growth of the Gross National Product. We realize what's important is that six trillion dollars changes hands in the United States every year—that's $6,000,000,000,000. If the big corporations are foundering so badly that they're getting less of it, that leaves more for you and me—lots more.

Why am I so confident? The 1990s are a time, in the words of one economist, of "hyper-change": that is, incredibly rapid shifts in consumer wants and needs. Later in this book, I'll go into the reasons why today's markets are so unpredictable, such as sophisticated technology that rapidly creates stunning new products and services, and the pervasiveness of cable television and other media that can create consumer demand for these new products and services almost overnight. But the important point to remember now is:

> In times of great change and economic chaos, there are always clear-cut winners and losers.

If you've been reading the business pages or the *Wall Street Journal* every day, you know who the losers are. But you may not realize that the winners will be people like you: those who don't just accept, but embrace change; who have conditioned themselves to seek out opportunities instead of excuses; and, most important of all, who understand that good, old-fashioned people skills are the key asset to achieving success in any area of life.

How can I be sure that these qualities will make people winners in these turbulent economic times? For the last twenty-two years I've had a terrific and profitable time riding the roller coaster of consumer demand in the most unpredictable of all businesses: fad products ranging from designer shoelaces to Batman T-shirts. Fads are by definition illogical and unpredictable (did anyone really need a Pet Rock?), and when one emerges the demand exceeds the supply overnight. When a fad fades, the demand disappears even more quickly—in 1989, I sold hundreds of thousands of Batman T-shirts in four months; in the fifth month, I couldn't have given them away. My company, Taylor Associates, has prospered because everyone, from our telephone salespeople to our 223 sales representatives in the field, has been trained to work in accordance with one key principle:

> Our survival depends on stocking, selling, and shipping TODAY what our customers want TODAY, not what they wanted yesterday or what a staff of M.B.A.'s or computers projected they'd want tomorrow.

While we grew and grew, we watched dozens of would-be competitors go bankrupt with warehouses full of merchandise from fads that used to be or never were.

How did I decide on the fad business? Most businesspeople I meet assume that I'm either a free spirit or some sort of cultural guru. The truth is that from my earliest days selling merchandise out of the trunk of my car I discovered that it was a lot easier to sell things that consumers really wanted than to convince people to buy something they didn't know they needed. It didn't bother me that one month that product could be T-shirts, the next month jewelry, the third month shoelaces. I concentrated on developing the people skills that brought success no matter what I sold. Eventually, I advanced to the point where I had developed a number of written principles by which I conducted my professional life.

Even when I took a few minutes to think about the future, I didn't foresee a time when consumer demand in nearly every business would be as volatile as it is in the fad business. When the economy became more turbulent, I began to think about writing a book that would help others prosper in these tough times. But I hesitated for a long time. The reason was that while I believed that my principles were valid for everyone in every type of work, I hadn't put my money where my mouth was by leaping into a totally unrelated field. The more I thought about it, the more I decided it would be interesting and exciting to put my theories to a practical test. Could I get a foothold in a tough, totally unrelated business in which I had no experience and was totally unknown? In other words, could I sell *myself* as effectively as I had sold T-shirts?

The culmination of that practical test took place in Chicago and Pittsburgh in June 1992 when I was part of the exclusive national radio broadcast team for the National Hockey League Stanley Cup finals and in Cooperstown, New York, on an August 1992 weekend when I hosted the 1992 Baseball Hall of Fame induction ceremonies for national radio. I had taped a radio interview with the then commissioner of Major League Baseball, Fay Vincent, on the beautiful veranda of the Otesaga Hotel before adjourning to the dining room for lunch. As I was leaving the restaurant, I ran into Mr. Vincent, who was coming into lunch. I asked the commissioner if he would be a guest on my show in the upcoming weeks. He handed me a card and said, "Stu, here's my home telephone number. Feel free to call me at home anytime."

The reason that this story is remarkable is that I'm not a well-known career broadcaster. In early 1991, at middle age, I had decided to make broadcasting, one of America's most fiercely competitive fields, the arena for my test. Other than having been interviewed by the press a few times, I had no broadcasting experience and no direct broadcasting contacts. I didn't want to buy a radio station or spend a dime to buy my way in. Instead, I decided to rely totally on the people skills I had developed in building my own business.

Three months later, I was the host of a weekly sports interview and talk show heard on 110 radio stations across the country on the American Radio Networks (that later expanded to more than 200 stations). In April 1991, I joined the Sports Final team, which included ex-major-league stars Bill Buckner and Rico Petrocelli, and NFL player Trevor Matich.

My assignment in Cooperstown in August 1992 was to set up interviews to fill the many hours of air time between Friday night and Sunday night. To do so, I had to compete with more than two hundred other media representatives from the TV networks, major newspapers, wire services, magazines, major city TV stations, and others. Between receptions, dinners, official ceremonies, and the Hall of Fame game, the inductees, the commissioner, the president of the leagues, and the baseball greats in attendance had very limited time for one-on-one interviews. I knew that at most I'd have a minute or two with each of these celebrities to sell myself and my network. The prospect could have been intimidating, but it wasn't. Although I was a broadcasting neophyte, I'd spent my lifetime selling myself to other people. After all, celebrities are people, too. I viewed my assignment not as a chore, but as a challenge, and I was anxious to begin.

The results exceeded my expectations. We fulfilled our commitment to the stations on our network by interviewing every important person in Cooperstown. I personally got the chance to share my boyhood baseball memories with Ted Williams and talk with Joe Garagiola. I felt like I'd survived an initiation rite, and my confidence was so high that I couldn't wait to get to the Football Hall of Fame ceremonies in Canton, Ohio, two weeks later.

On the long drive back to Boston from Cooperstown, I was surprised to find how much I'd impressed my colleagues, some of whom had been sports broadcasters for decades. That's when I made yet another decision: I would write the book my friends had been urging me to tackle for years.

So here they are: the twenty-four principles on which I've based my success. To use these principles to take advantage of the tremendous opportunities available in the 1990s, you only have to do one thing: accept the fact that the only limits to what you can achieve are the limits you place on yourself. Once you take responsibility for your own success, you'll be a true entrepreneur who is bound to achieve in the years to come.

How to Turn Trends Into Fortunes

A Case Study

The thing always happens that you really believe in;
and the belief in a thing makes it happen.
                                        —Frank Lloyd Wright

This book is all about taking the initiative to make yourself a success—starting today. Before I explain the twenty-four principles that can make it all happen for you, I want to show you how seizing an opportunity can lead us to a significant career gain.

In the summer of 1977, Taylor Associates was one of the largest distributors of posters, plaques, incense, novelty jewelry, and similar products in New England. I also had productive relationships with sales representatives in New York City, Philadelphia, and other major cities on the eastern seaboard. My ambition was to become a national distributor, but I had been thwarted in several attempts to expand beyond the East Coast. The primary reason was that none of my existing product lines was unique or unusual, and I couldn't tempt manufacturers' representatives to handle products similar to those they could get shipped more quickly from distributors in their own geographical area. I wasn't the only one to face this problem—there were no national distributors. But I didn't let the fact that it hadn't been done prevent me from believing it could be done.

Then, out of the blue, came the first in a series of events that was to give me the opportunity to achieve that goal nearly overnight. In New York on a business trip, I was watching television in my hotel room when news came of Elvis Presley's death. Realizing that there would be a huge demand for Elvis memorabilia, I immediately picked up the phone to call Jim Layhew, the manufacturer's representative who handled my products in New York. Another company he handled printed Elvis posters. I asked for and received New England distribution rights. We were selling

Elvis posters right after the newspapers announcing his death hit the stands. In a few days, we shipped thousands. Then the Presley estate sold exclusive licensing rights to Factors, Inc., and we had to terminate sales. Still, it had been a lucrative venture for Jim Layhew, the poster manufacturer, and Taylor Associates.

A few weeks later, I got a call from the president of the poster company, who had been impressed with our quick, aggressive action on the Presley merchandise. He invited me to New York to discuss distributing posters for *Saturday Night Fever*. I thought he said "Saturday Night Live." But he went on to explain that *Saturday Night Fever* was a movie with a disco score by the Bee Gees and starring John Travolta, who had become a star in the TV series, "Welcome Back, Kotter." He went on to say that Paramount had big promotional plans for the film, and he thought I'd be interested in a piece of the action.

I was. Recent movies such as *Jaws* and *Rocky* had generated very substantial poster sales after their releases. Paramount planned to surpass those sales through the then-unique technique of promoting the movie before its release. It sounded good to me.

I met Jim Layhew and the poster licensee at a screening held in the Gulf + Western building in Manhattan. Even in its unedited three-hour version, *Saturday Night Fever* had an enormous impact on me and the rest of the audience. I could sense that the movie would be a big hit. As for John Travolta, I was reminded of the impact made by Marlon Brando in *The Wild One* and by James Dean in *Rebel Without a Cause*. I was certain Travolta was the next cult hero.

As we left the building and took a cab to lunch, plans were spinning through my head. Almost out of the blue, a window of opportunity was about to open briefly, the kind of opportunity I looked for every day of my life. It was up to me, and me alone, to squeeze through that window before it closed.

A few minutes later we were seated in a restaurant and ordering lunch. The offer I expected arrived along with the appetizers—the exclusive New England distributorship for *Fever* posters and fold-out prints. For his part in arranging the original contact between the poster company and me, Jim Layhew would receive a 2 percent override on all my sales. I nodded politely, then asked Jim to join me in the men's room.

When we got inside, I told Jim that I was about to ask the

poster licensee to give me exclusive *national* distribution rights for all posters and prints. Jim told me I was stark, raving mad. He pointed out that I had no sales coverage in 80 percent of the United States. Calmly, I pointed out that if I succeeded, he would receive a 2 percent override on all national sales. As dollar signs registered in his eyes, he agreed to back me. But I could see that he thought I had a snowball's chance in hell of succeeding.

I understood Jim's doubt, but I was not about to let that stop me. I'd learned early in life that if you wait for the most beautiful girl in school to ask you to dance, you'll be a wallflower all your life. If I was going to be a national distributor, I had to do it myself.

I made my pitch to the poster licensee and encountered the initial skepticism I expected. But gradually I began to win him over. Now, I'm a very good salesman, and I'm sure my argument about the cost-effectiveness and efficiency of shipping to one distributor instead of several scored some points. But rational arguments alone wouldn't have won the day. Rather, I think the poster licensee was overwhelmed by my enthusiasm for the film and for his merchandise. I could almost see him thinking that if I could transfer that enthusiasm to a sales force, he'd sell a lot more posters. So, by the time dessert arrived, I'd locked up the national distribution rights.

We shook hands on the deal, then I headed for LaGuardia Airport to catch a shuttle back to Boston. In the cab, I thought about the next step—actually recruiting a national sales force. I stopped at the gate to make some telephone calls. I wanted directories of manufacturers' representatives and showrooms across the country on my desk the next morning.

On the plane, I planned my strategy. My new contract gave me temporary leverage, and I planned to use it. I knew I'd have little problem getting very capable people to handle *Saturday Night Fever* merchandise. Word of Paramount's promotional efforts would make it a hot property. So I was going to insist that every manufacturers' rep who wanted *Fever* posters was going to have to agree to take on my entire product line. Once again, I knew that I wouldn't get what I wanted if I didn't take the initiative.

The next morning I was on the phone, networking to get a list of the top people. Within thirty-six hours, I had scheduled appointments with all of them during a whirlwind twelve-city, five-day barnstorming tour. My schedule was so tight that I made my Detroit presentation in the airport waiting area in front of a couple dozen reps and about fifty curious people waiting for planes. When I finished my presentation, I was startled at receiving a standing ovation.

Most reps said they'd take the *Saturday Night Fever* line; as planned, my response was, "You'll have to take my entire line." In the end, I'd heard enough complaining and kicking and screaming to last a lifetime. I also got every rep I wanted except one to agree to my deal. I had become a national distributor in one calendar week.

Once again, I couldn't rest on my laurels. I had to actually sell the posters. As part of the contract with the licensee, I was obligated to order twenty-five thousand dollars in posters up front—not a lot of money today, but a fortune to me back then. Those posters, rolled in polyethylene tubes and ready to ship in point-of-purchase display units were stacked in my warehouse. I sent a flood of sales materials to my reps, then I waited for the onslaught of orders to arrive.

I waited, and waited, and waited. I received exactly one order, from a drugstore chain buyer who, I think, felt sorry for me. No one else was willing to speculate that a movie would generate merchandise sales, no matter how much prerelease hype the studio generated. Paramount was dismayed. There aren't words to describe how I felt.

The only thing that snapped me out of my misery was being invited to the New York premiere of the movie. I was thrilled to sit a few seats from Farah Fawcett, and to meet John Travolta and the rest of the cast at a lavish party at Tavern on the Green. I just hoped I hadn't paid twenty-five thousand dollars for the privilege of hobnobbing with the rich and famous.

My big chance to get rid of that inventory was the Transworld Variety Exhibit, one of the nation's premier order-writing shows. That year's event was scheduled for Chicago in January 1978, just after the movie's release. I had one of the most spectacular booths at the show because Paramount had provided me with an actual electric movie billboard for my booth, along with music from the soundtrack. I hoped the trade show would open with a blizzard of orders.

Instead, it opened with a blizzard—a foot of snow that closed the airports. Only a handful of people who had arrived in town the day before wandered the aisles of the show. But just when things looked bleakest, a smooth-talking Chicago-based salesman, the kind of guy I normally dislike at first sight, walked into my booth and announced, "Bullshit walks, money talks—I want *Saturday Night Fever*." I could have kissed him.

I had hardly arrived back home when the orders started pouring in. That aggressive Chicago salesman was hopscotching around the country selling to large chains such as Ben Franklin, Osco Drug, and JCPenney. I sold out my initial order in a few days, and freight company trucks arrived every day with new supplies. I was on top of the world.

Business stayed red-hot through the month of February. But I was increasingly preoccupied with my next big decision—when to pull the plug. Riding the crest of a fad is a huge high, but the crash can be a killer. If I stopped ordering merchandise too soon, I would be losing big profits; if demand stopped when I had a warehouse full of merchandise, most of the profits I'd earned would be wiped out.

The only solution was to stay in constant touch with the market. I left the processing of orders to others and I spent every waking moment working the telephone, calling retailers directly to monitor their day-to-day sales. After a couple of weeks, I discovered that sales were dropping off at some outlets in New York and Los Angeles. I stopped ordering new merchandise and emptied my warehouse. A few days later, the sales of *Saturday Night Fever* merchandise virtually ceased. It was so sudden, it was as if the front page of every newspaper in the country had ordered people not to buy. But I didn't care.

A couple weeks later, my wife and I were treated to a vacation in Aruba by the poster licensee. As I rested on the plane, I enjoyed a deep sense of satisfaction. It wasn't just that I'd made a lot of money and developed a national sales force, although those had been major goals of mine. What was more important was that my success had come about because I had taken the initiative and done it myself. I had spotted an opportunity, dared to take a risk, moved with great speed and passion, and had persevered over temporary obstacles. As a result, I was on top of the world.

See the Field
Lessons in Spotting Opportunities From Joe Montana and My Dad

The people who get on in this world are the people who get up and look for the circumstances they want and, if they can't find them, make them.

—George Bernard Shaw

Ever find yourself thinking that the reason you haven't achieved more of your goals is that you haven't been lucky? Well, I've always thought that the best definition of *luck* was "the reason for the success of someone you don't like." I've found that people who take responsibility for their own success and pursue their dreams sixty hours a week tend to be a lot luckier than people who work thirty hours a week and wait passively for their ship to come in.

However, not long ago, I realized that I had been the beneficiary of one extraordinary bit of good fortune that had nothing to do with how hard I'd worked over the years. That piece of luck, which played a crucial role in my development as a person and a businessman, was being Bert and Esther Taylor's son. Either through inheritance or osmosis, Bert passed along to me an attitude that has been the single most important factor in my success. Ironically, it wasn't until January 1990, a few months after my father's death, that I realized exactly what that contribution had been.

I remember sitting with a few friends watching the San Francisco Forty-Niners rout the Denver Broncos in Super Bowl XXIV. I'd always admired John Elway, a good quarterback with great physical skills. But that day, Joe Montana provided every football fan with a vivid lesson of the difference between good and great.

9

As he marched his team up and down the field, Montana demonstrated what seemed to be a sixth sense that allowed him to counter a blitz with a screen pass or send a receiver into a narrow gap in the Denver coverage. By the second half, the Broncos seemed dazed, as if they'd been the victim of a spell cast by Montana.

Of course, there is absolutely nothing psychic or magical about Joe Montana. Rather, his greatness comes from a carefully and deliberately developed confidence that allows him to continue to take in, process, and act on information even in the most pressure-packed situations. As the clock ticks away, he seems to become calmer and more confident, which makes him even more alert to both opportunities and danger signals—a cornerback cheating a half step toward the sideline in anticipation of an out pattern; a safety slightly favoring one leg; a linebacker shifting his weight forward in preparation for a blitz. As he evaluates each bit of information, Montana constantly modifies his game plan to produce big play after big play.

This ability to "see the field" is as important in quarterbacking your career as it is in quarterbacking a football team. If opportunities were obvious, everyone would be a millionaire. If you want to be successful, you have to be constantly alert to the most subtle signs of opportunity. The chance you've been waiting for can come at any time and in the most unexpected way.

The number of opportunities for people whose primary capital is hard work and desire, increases in hard economic times, when many established businesses founder or fail. No one in his or her right mind welcomes recessions and all the hardships they bring to many people. But I was fortunate to learn early in life that remaining optimistic when everyone else is gloomy can pay rich rewards. No better example of this exists than how my father, the quintessential do-it-now person, got started in his career in the depths of the Great Depression.

Bert Taylor grew up one of seven children on a self-sufficient family farm in Maine. His enterprising parents had scraped and saved enough to build Taylor Farms, one of the few kosher hotels outside of New York State. In the 1920s, the hotel and the Taylor family prospered as it was packed with patrons from New York and Boston who came to see some of the top entertainers of the day, such as Eddie Duchin on the piano. Unfortunately, both the hotel and the farm were lost in the depression. Like many other young men of that time, Bert packed his few belongings in a satchel and went to the big city—in this case, Boston—in search of opportunity.

For a few months, Bert scratched out a meager living doing occasional odd jobs. One morning, he was walking down a street on his way to some much-needed work unloading a furniture van when he passed two men in the midst of a violent argument. One of them, a merchant going out of business, had made a deal to sell the entire contents of his store to the second man. The buyer had tried to renegotiate at the last moment, enraging the seller. As Bert Taylor passed, the merchant grabbed his arm and offered to sell him the merchandise at half the previously negotiated price. In addition, the merchant offered to finance the sale.

Bert didn't know a thing about buying and selling merchandise. What he knew was that he couldn't pay the rent on his room or eat for the next week without the money he would earn unloading furniture. But Bert didn't let these intense pressures affect his attitude. He knew, instantly, that this street argument momentarily opened a door. Without hesitating, he shook hands on the deal, went out into the street, and flagged down a passing truck. He offered the driver the change he had in his pocket to deliver the merchant's goods to his tiny room. He inventoried what he'd bought, then systematically worked his way up one Boston street and down the next, calling on every store he passed. Ten days later, he'd sold everything and paid off his debt.

The handsome profit he made from that first load of merchandise launched Bert's career as a buyer and seller of distressed and surplus goods. Some of my earliest, and fondest, memories are of accompanying my father on long car trips through New England. He would stop at factory after factory, store after store, warehouse after warehouse, asking if they had anything to sell. Of all the lessons I learned from my dad, the most important was that an opportunity could come along any time, anywhere, involving anything. We came home with everything from hunting knives to canned Salisbury steak. No matter what it was, my father managed to sell it for a profit.

Like Joe Montana, my father cultivated the ability to see the field. He awoke every morning telling himself, "Somewhere out there is another opportunity for me to find today." It wasn't that he was a pie-in-the-sky optimist. Rather, from practical experience he had discovered that the harder he looked, the more opportunities he found, even in the worst of economic times.

My mother's attitude was equally positive. Both of my parents inspired me to face life with energy and determination, even when I was a teenager. My brother Jason, who is four years older, also served as a role model during my early years. When it came time for me to go to college, I wanted to show my parents and my brother how much I appreciated their examples by paying my own way. I didn't have to—I'd never lacked for anything growing up and the money was there for tuition if I needed it. But I wanted to.

The problem was, how to do it? A part-time job at the $1.25 minimum wage would only bring me pocket money, and borrowing capital from my father was not part of my self-imposed ground rules. So I decided to apply what I'd learned and look for an unconventional opportunity. I investigated and discarded several ideas. Then, one day, I heard about a new contest sponsored by one of Boston's most popular radio stations. Every hour the station would announce a randomly selected license plate number. The owner of the vehicle then had one hour from the time of the announcement to show up at the station and claim a cash prize ranging from $50 to $250.

The contest signaled "gold mine" to me. I enlisted the support of my mother, who agreed to listen to the station all day. Once an hour, I would call her to get the new plate number. Then I'd call the state registry of motor vehicles, do some fast talking, and convince them to give me the name of the owner of that plate. After obtaining the owner's telephone number from information, I'd try to persuade him or her to hurry to the station to claim the prize. When I was successful, I arranged to meet the winner outside the station to collect my "finder's fee." Reminiscent of "The Millionaire"—a popular TV show of the 1950s—I cautioned the winner not to reveal the source of information at the risk of disqualification. I soon became a master of disguise donning all kinds of clothing and hats when I met my clients so that station personnel wouldn't associate me with the parade of winners.

Eventually, the much-higher-than-anticipated percentage of winners caused the station to cancel the contest—but not before I had managed to earn several thousand dollars, more than enough to pay my tuition. I enjoyed the feeling of intense satisfaction I derived from my innovative entrepreneurship even more than the money. The thrill of finding a money-making opportunity others had overlooked inspired me for decades to come.

There isn't a business in the world in which the ability to "see the field" can't lead to success. For example, Peter Lynch, who built Fidelity Investments' Magellan Fund into the largest and most successful mutual fund in the United States, came home from work one night to find his wife exclaiming about the convenience of purchasing a new brand of stockings in little plastic containers on a supermarket rack. Lynch discovered that before the introduction of L'eggs, women had to make a special trip to a hosiery shop to buy stockings. He did a little research, then made an investment that produced one of the highest returns in the history of his fund.

Another unlooked-for product came out of the 3M company's research into new adhesives. A researcher discovered by accident that one of the experimental compounds was perfect for sticking removable notes on reports and other documents. Pads of these handy little sticky notes soon circulated through the executive offices. When a marketing executive noticed, 3M had a brand-new product that was a smash commercial success—Post-it Notes.

The fad business boasts a wealth of success stories based on people seeing new possibilities where others hadn't. For example, a Philadelphia marine architect and naval engineer named Richard James was repairing a piece of equipment one day when a torsion spring fell off the table. As James watched the spring bounce back and forth, he suddenly got the idea that it might be amusing if he could get it to "walk" down the stairs. When he introduced his modified spring, now called a Slinky, at Gimbel's department store, he sold one every twenty-five seconds. Millions are still sold every year, forty-six years later.

Of course, not every idea turns out to be as successful as the Slinky. I only buy a handful of the thousands of products presented to me in my office or at trade shows. Still, I carefully weigh every sales pitch. In my mind, I try to look for a reason to say yes instead of no. The day I lose my enthusiasm for unexpected opportunities will be the day I retire.

But I don't expect that to happen. My father worked right up until his death, relishing the excitement of every new fad. Joe

Montana will eventually retire when his physical skills erode, but I suspect that he'll move on to excellence in another career. Learning to see the field is like slipping on the colored glasses in a 3-D movie—suddenly, opportunities seem to stand out everywhere.

Still not convinced undiscovered opportunities are everywhere? Then go to the library and find "The Verger," a short story by the great writer Somerset Maugham. The hero of the tale is the verger of a London church who is fired after more than twenty years on the job when the new pastor learns he is unable to read and write. Depressed, the man wanders for hours through the streets. Eventually, he gets the urge to have a cigarette, but he walks many blocks down one main street without finding a tobacco shop.

A few days later, he goes back to that street and uses his life savings to rent a tiny store and stock it with tobacco products. The store is extremely successful, and soon he starts wandering the city looking for another long street without a tobacco shop. In a few years, he owns a chain of profitable shops. One day, he is making a large bank deposit when the bank manager asks him to read and sign some paperwork. The banker is astounded when the man tells him he is unable to read.

"My good man," the banker says, "you've accumulated a fortune. Do you have any idea what you might have been if you could only read?"

The man replied, "Yes, I do. I would be the verger of St. Stephen's Church."

No better lesson exists that opportunity doesn't come just from education, but from attitude.

Some Things to Think About

- Buy a brand-new notebook and write down a new idea or opportunity that comes to mind every day. At the end of the month, go back over your notebook. Some pages won't make any sense, and some will seem silly or impossible. But chances are one or two will make you some money.

- Quarterbacks like Joe Montana spend hours and hours studying films of their opponents. You should make a habit of reading the business pages of your daily newspaper, the *Wall Street Journal, Forbes, Business Week*, and magazines aimed at entrepreneurs and small businesspeople, such as

Success and *Inc.* They're filled with case studies of people who have translated opportunities into thriving companies.

- Read new publications, listen to new radio stations, watch different TV news shows. Buy out-of-town newspapers every so often. The change in perspective will help you learn to look at things in new ways.

Set the Woods on Fire
The Best Way to Promote Yourself is to Beat the Bush, Instead of Beating Around It

> If you want to win anything—a race, your self, your life—
> you have to go a little berserk.
>
> —George Sheehan

I'm not a deer hunter, but I have several friends who are. From their stories, I know the time, expense, and effort they expend every year stalking through the cold woods to bag their buck. One buddy told me that he has calculated his venison steaks cost him about fifty dollars a pound. He doesn't mind, because he hunts deer for sport.

However, if he were hunting deer to feed his family for the winter, stalking deer one by one could lead to starvation. He'd be far better off using a more efficient method, such as setting the woods on fire and picking off the herd that comes fleeing out the other side.

Now, I know that literally setting the woods on fire is not a legal or moral way to hunt. But it is a perfect metaphor for the best way to make a name for yourself in business. Every day that you don't approach your job as if your survival depends on what you accomplish that day is, in my mind, a day on which you'll lose ground. If you're not hungry enough, someone else will be.

Unfortunately, most companies are staffed with people who don't have a passion for their work. When you work with these people, it's hard not to absorb their attitudes toward their jobs. Treating work like a hobby becomes an ingrained habit—a dangerous habit that's hard to break.

I almost fell into this trap on my first serious job. I attended Northeastern University which had—and still has—a nationally recognized cooperative work/study program. As an experimental psychology major, I worked on academic research assignments during my first three years. But in my senior year, I finally left the rats and Skinner boxes behind for an applied psychology assignment with Teaching Systems Inc., which produced sales manuals for industry and educational institutions written in programmed instruction form; a psychological technique of stimulus/response reinforcement.

After graduation, I decided to stay with Teaching Systems. However, my permanent job involved writing and editing manuals rather than interviewing and consulting as I'd done on my work/study job. I soon became frustrated, so I formulated a plan that I hoped would give my boss the incentive to use me as a consultant.

Almost all of our company's contracts were with companies headquartered on the East Coast. I took vacation time, flew to California, and spent a week making sales presentations to Carnation, Standard Oil of California, Max Factor, and several smaller corporations. The response I received from these potential clients was very encouraging. I could hardly wait until I returned to Boston to tell my boss.

He listened, thanked me politely, and then did nothing. I was astonished and dismayed that he refused to pursue any of the leads I had created. To me, it was like a clean-up hitter taking a 3–0 fastball down the middle with the bases loaded. At that very early stage of my business career, I knew I was facing a turning point. If I accepted my boss's attitude toward doing business, I was sure I'd eventually adopt it as my own. If I didn't accept it, I had to quit.

I left. I decided that I never could or never would give anyone else the chance to turn down business I created. If I was going to do it myself, I was going to do it my way. The only problem was that I didn't know exactly what else I wanted to do, or could do. My only capital was my attitude and energy.

To pass the time, I worked with my father for a while. Then I met a delightful man named Matt Gonsalves. Matt was a craftsman who imported Hummel prints from Germany and laminated them on pine plaques. He had laboriously built up a small business, but he hated sales work. Our meeting was a marriage made in heaven. Matt was so eager to have someone else sell his plaques that he agreed to let me pay him after I'd collected from customers. I was in business.

The next day, I began setting the woods on fire. I loaded up the trunk of my car before dawn, drew a route on a road map, and started out. I stopped at every single store on that route that might be remotely interested in carrying Matt's plaques. I'd introduce myself to the manager or owner, engage in some pleasant chat, show my wares, then leave with a handshake and a promise to return the next week. Working from dawn to dusk, I kept those promises.

Within a few weeks, I had established a series of routes that included all of my existing customers (a small but respectable number) and my best prospects (a much larger number). At the end of each business day, I'd come home at eight or nine o'clock to prepare invoices, log in my payments, and calculate how much I had made that day. Those figures increased almost every week.

The next step in building my new business was to add to my product line. I picked up Gary & Gretchen, Still Life, and Currier and Ives plaques, which gave me added minutes with buyers and added sales. Then a high-school friend of mine, Jay Desantis, introduced me to artist Bob Kennedy. Bob and his brothers, who called themselves Kennedy Studios, produced lithographed prints of historical Boston sites. They sold these prints either ready to frame or framed. The Kennedys were prepared to expand and I was ready to sell more than I could fit into the trunk of my car every day. I agreed to sell their products and they agreed to let me use their facilities to ship all of my daily orders by United Parcel Service.

By beating the bushes for customers and for products to sell, I built a very nice business. I did approximately $12,500 in business my first year, $33,000 the second, $66,000 the third year, and by the fourth year my sales reached six figures. I didn't start with a dime of capital and I didn't have some other special advantage conferred upon me by a certain kind of training or college degree. What I had was the right attitude—carving out a career by doing it myself.

You don't have to be a salesperson to set the woods on fire every day. Sam Walton became the richest man in America because he spent every available minute visiting Wal-Mart stores to make sure his customers were being treated properly. Ray Kroc insisted that every McDonald's executive spend at least one day a year working behind the counter in one of their restaurants as part of a quality-control program unprecedented in the fast-food industry. Stephen King became one of the wealthiest authors in the United States by locking himself in a room with a typewriter from nine to five, seven days a week, year after year.

You have to look for ways to beat the bushes in your line of work. I had to change my way of doing business when I started to grow. In my fourth year, I took on an exciting line of stunning color aerial photographs of such picturesque Northeast sites as Marblehead Harbor, Boston, Rockport, Nantucket, and Martha's Vineyard. At the same time, Kennedy Studios expanded into peace, political, and environmentally oriented posters and bumper stickers. These new products gave me access to the buyers from such prestigious department store chains as Jordan Marsh and Filenes. I also began receiving inquiries from New York City and other areas outside of New England.

This increase in business was exciting, but it presented me with a problem. I wouldn't have had enough hours in the day to make all my calls even if I had the Starship *Enterprise* to beam me back and forth. The solution was to increase my contacts with both retailers and manufacturers by participating in trade shows. My first was the 1970 Cape Cod gift show at the Sheraton in Hyannis, Massachusetts. I showed a little savvy by paying a little extra for a strategically located corner booth.

The show opened my eyes to a whole new world. I talked to more people in a day than I could have called on in a month. I also had the incredible luck to be assigned a booth next to a fascinating and funny man named Maury Simonds, who became both a friend and mentor to me. Maury and I teamed up to take adjacent booths for upcoming shows in Connecticut, Vermont, and Maine.

Even more important, Maury alerted me to an opportunity that became a turning point in the growth of my business. In 1970, a number of large companies formed the Gift and Decorative Accessories Association. This association rented a building in the Boston area that would house twelve showrooms and be open to retailers all year round. The founding companies took eleven of the twelve. Maury Simonds urged me to share the last show-room with him.

While I was on the phone with Maury, the idea of taking on what was then a substantial monthly rent almost made me say no. Then I realized that a showroom in the Gift and Decorative Accessories Center in Burlington, Massachusetts, would give me exposure to many more customers than I could possibly contact in person. I couldn't let my reluctance to take on overhead overcome my far more important belief that the only way to do business was to set the woods on fire. Procrastination would have been fatal. I said yes to Maury, and we snapped up the last space. The remorse of my competitors still rings in my ears. Today, the expanded Gift Center is home to the showrooms of more than a hundred companies, and many more wait years to get to the top of the waiting list.

I relate this story because I have become increasingly puzzled by the low priority many companies and businesspeople place on old-fashioned selling. For example, IBM has cut its sales force to the point where a salesperson often takes months to make a first courtesy call on a new CEO taking over the helm of an important customer. That's an open invitation to aggressive competitors. That's why in the electronics industry, in the fad and giftware industry, and in many other fields, American companies are losing ground to companies based in the Far East. Asian compan-ies are staffed by people who work longer hours, make more calls, and respond more quickly.

Too many American companies today are run by executives who organize their time like a manufacturer's representative I met at many of my first gift shows, a man I'll call Arnold. Arnold, a very bright man who had earned an M.B.A, disdained what he viewed as the haphazard way in which most salespeople went about their business. He applied statistical analysis to his product lines and came up with a computer printout that allotted his sales time to the sales volume generated by each account. He carefully developed one, five, and ten year sales projections for every product in every line he represented. At one gift show, he proudly came up to Maury Simonds and me to announce that he was projecting a 27.7 percent increase in sales in the next ten months.

Maury turned to me and said, "Kid, are our sales up 27.7

percent or down 27.7 percent?" Arnold gave us a withering look and hurried off. A year later, Arnold went bankrupt. What he had forgotten to factor into his plan was that he was spending more and more time massaging numbers and less and less time massaging customers.

I don't mean to imply that sophisticated financial analysis has no place in corporations. But when it comes to results, business is like baseball—statistics are valuable, but what wins games is stepping up to the plate and getting base hits. The more swings you take, the more hits you'll get.

Some Things to Think About

- Almost nobody I've met knows exactly how many contacts he or she makes in the course of a day. So keep a log and total it every night. Increasing that total by ten contacts a week will produce dramatic results.

- Stop thinking about contacts as formal meetings or sales presentations. When I have a spare moment, I often pick up the phone just to ask, "What's new?" "How's business?" or "How is your family?" I haven't met very many people, even busy people, who don't like to talk about themselves when there is a friendly voice on the line.

- Talk to yourself. I keep a pocket tape recorder next to me while I'm driving. I use the time to think about new ways to set the woods on fire. Then I listen to the tape later to modify or correct myself before I try the ideas out on anyone else.

Go West, Young Man
Reflections on the Hypothesis That a Rat Moves Faster the Closer It Gets to the Goal

The great thing in this world is not so much where we are, but in what direction we are moving.
—Oliver Wendell Holmes

I still make use of some of the principles I learned in my experimental psychology classes in college. One that's always stuck in my mind has a rather imposing name, Hull's Goal Gradient Hypothesis. But behind this jargon is a valuable concept. Now, you don't need a psychology course to figure out that you need to provide some sort of reward or goal to make a rat work at figuring out a maze or perform another kind of task. However, a man named Hull discovered that rats moved faster the closer they got to their goals. The anticipation of more immediate rewards increased their motivation.

As individuals, and collectively, as a nation, we conform to Hull's hypothesis, too. If you study American history, you'll discover that historians believe that the idea of the frontier was crucial to the growth of the United States as a world power. In the eighteenth and nineteenth centuries, every American knew that there were new lands and new opportunities just over the horizon. Reaching those new lands wasn't an abstract idea or an impossible dream—even if you weren't going there, you knew lots of people just like you who were. The optimism about the future produced by the frontier spurred the entire nation to unprecedented growth and prosperity.

Unfortunately, the frontier is gone. In fact, our own land has become the land of opportunity for other optimistic and aggressive nations with something to prove. With the exception of the recent war in the Persian Gulf and the humanitarian aid mission to Somalia, it has been a long time since the American people pulled together toward a common, attainable goal.

But the subject of this book isn't politics—it's your success in life. To be successful, you need a frontier—the right kind of goal. Goals that are too big—becoming a millionaire, dating Madonna, or, in my case, playing third base for the Red Sox—are the stuff of daydreams. The chances of reaching these goals are so remote that they don't provide sufficient motivation. On the other hand, mundane or easily attainable goals are fine for maintaining the status quo, but don't provide sufficient incentive for you to make the extra effort to get ahead.

What I've always tried to do is set a goal that's the equivalent of the frontier—a big, exciting new opportunity that's just over the horizon. The first time I remember doing this in my career ended up with me literally following the advice, "Go west, young man."

The early 1970s were a time of social upheaval and change. On the downside, there was an infusion of drugs into our culture and the Vietnam War was still raging. Head shops, hot pants, smile faces, and psychedelic designs were in vogue and "mod shops" were springing up all over the country, featuring such items as incense, black-light posters and bulbs, patches, and switchplate covers. This was a time when fads were developing in the mountains and valleys of California and sweeping across the country from west to east. I entertained thoughts of going to the California Gift Show, and one day a Cape Cod merchant convinced me that I should hesitate no longer.

My values were not to be compromised. While several of my contemporaries went on to make their fortunes with pipes and cigarette papers, I decided to go the mod shop route. In doing this, I selected items that I felt met socially acceptable standards. It was the genuine beginnings of a continuing fad period—not merely characterized by an occasional phenomenon such as a Hula-Hoop or a Slinky, but an ongoing evolution of products molded into a myriad of motifs.

My first West Coast connection was with a Los Angeles based company—Rabbi Burnbaum, Inc. RBI manufactured stick, cone, and powder incense of the same name. This was the first bonafide fad I encountered, and I was determined to make the most of the opportunity at hand. I desperately wanted to put together a product potpourri consisting of many items and bring this package back to the Northeast. My plan was to pick out enough items to offer a comprehensive sole-source merchandise program to stores.

The norm had been for stores to buy their merchandise from several different manufacturers' representatives. The role of each rep was to write orders through many companies. My single-point distribution center philosophy has been the mainstay of Taylor Associates ever since.

They say that clothes make the man. However, in sales, the man's clothes must coordinate with the product. I generally dressed casually in jeans and an open-collar shirt and was easily identified with the product line I sold. Had I been a salesman for crystal, glass, and fine wood products, I would have projected a more formal image and articulated my sales presentation in that mold. I have always tried to relate to buyers and vendors in terms they were comfortable with, being conscious of neither talking nor dressing up or down to them. This basic principle applies in every business.

As a result of my initial California trip I was able to add posters, black-light bulbs, decals, and switchplate covers to my product line. Other major acquisitions were incense, parchment scrolls, and mini black-light posters. I held a monopoly on these items for quite a long time.

The catch of the day was incense. Like food, it was consumable and therefore a terrific resale item. Burn it and replace it. Because of the worsening drug scene, the odor of incense became associated with covering up the smell of marijuana smoke. In spite of this, its market acceptance continued to grow. Demographics actually showed the typical incense consumer to be a thirty-five-year-old housewife with two children.

Rabbi Burnbaum was having production problems, and one day I received a telephone call from Rick Barry of the Olfactory Corporation in Los Angeles informing me that because of the reported difficulties with Rabbi Burnbaum he would like to meet with me at the upcoming National Fashion and Boutique Show to discuss a possible working relationship. Our meeting took place at the old McAlpin Hotel in New York City.

Rick Barry, a California hippie in appearance, with his more conservative associate, Rich Bandatt, negotiated with me for three hours to reach an agreement. I've never been as hard-nosed since; I demanded low prices, free merchandise displays, free freight, and the key to Barry's vault. I remember Rick shaking his head in disbelief and utter frustration saying, "Hey, man, that's the last time I'll ever deal with Stu Taylor." Rick and I are still dealing today, some twenty years later.

I remember with a chuckle an incident that occurred during a subsequent trip to California, when I introduced Rick Barry to my old Northeastern University college buddy, Dave Buonagurio. Dave was then a New York stock broker who always dressed in a three-piece suit. He was quite a character in his own right. Dave was an artist at mesmerizing people with his 200-word-per-minute machine gun speech. I was curiously awaiting the exchange that would follow their introduction. So, with my hands placed behind each of their heads, I put them nose to nose and waited. Laid-back Rick slowly drawled, "Hey Man, what sign are you?" Dave rapidly retorted, "Episcopalian."

With Rabbi Burnbaum and Olfactory in my growing line, I toyed with the idea of cornering the market by creating my own competition. Incense use was growing at a rapid rate and I wanted to grow with it.

The Hare Krishnas were producing an exceptionally high quality incense called Spiritual Sky Scented Products, although their management was not Krishna operated. Len Kurtz, the man in charge, set me up as a distributor. I than added two other name brands—Excelsior and Primo. These were followed up with three additional lines that enabled me to gain control of a large segment of the market. If this were a poker game, I would have been holding a full house. I resisted the egocentric temptation to package incense under my own name and instead stayed with the advertised brands. It was clear even at that early juncture what a destructive driving force ego could be.

So many entrepreneurs exit from the business almost as quickly as they start because of the absence of a pragmatic approach. Private labeling, as it is known—having your own brand name product—is a popular and innovative marketing technique. At that point, however, it would not have worked well with incense. The popular brand names were in such high demand that it was almost impossible to compete head to head with them. Since stores did not want to carry the same brand of incense as their local competition, I had the perfect solution. Instead of each store buying from a different company, many bought from me, acquiring an equal quality product in each store. I was my own competition. I have employed this technique successfully time and time again. If the retailer was going to buy incense from someone, shouldn't that someone be me?

The point is that ambition does not mean boosting one's own ego. The rewards of racing toward new frontiers are financial and personal. Seeking fame, as an end in itself, is pointless—unless your personal role model is Zsa Zsa Gabor.

I've always been a big admirer of people who built extraordinarily successful businesses, then left to start off all over again exploring a new frontier. These include men like:

- The brilliant Steve Jobs, who left Apple to develop the revolutionary Next computer.
- James Robinson, who sold his Chicago-based Subaru distributorship and founded Morgan Creek Productions, an independent film company that has made hits like *Young Guns, Major League,* and *Robin Hood.*
- Major League baseball player Joe Garagiola, who turned himself into a TV personality and motivational speaker after hanging up his cleats.

I mention these men because you're likely to have heard of them, not because their goals should be yours. All of us need a frontier that is just out of reach, not pie in the sky. For example, I greatly admire a woman I know who built a substantial business out of desperate adversity. She and her husband had just moved into a new home when the youngest of their two daughters was diagnosed with leukemia. A week later, her husband lost his job. Saving her home and paying her daughter's medical bills became her obsession. The only way she could think of to earn money quickly was to turn her house into a day-care center. With her husband's help, she obtained the necessary licenses, converted most of her living space into child-care rooms, and started recruiting children. Almost overnight she and her staff were caring for fifty children a day and she was paying her bills.

But she didn't stop there, even after her husband found a new job and her daughter conquered her illness. She converted her day-care business into the area's largest nursery school in order to cut down on the hours that her home would be used for business. Then she decided to use her "extra" time to become a consultant for others who wanted to enter the day-care business. She formed a second company, sought out speaking engagements, and gradually got more and more jobs. Eventually, she was named to the board of directors of the National Association of Child Care Consultants.

As I write this, she's moved on to yet another frontier. She has just opened the first facility of what she envisions as a national network of pilot day-care centers that can serve as training sites for entrepreneurs who want to get into this burgeoning field. I wouldn't want to bet against her succeeding. I also wouldn't want to bet against her coming up with a new goal when this one is accomplished.

As I've already mentioned in the introduction to this book, I have no intentions of resting on my laurels, either. Because I achieved most of my goals in the fad business, I've moved on to broadcasting, writing, and motivational speaking. I thrive on the adrenaline that comes from rolling out of bed each day to meet a challenge I've imposed on myself. There are vast opportunities out there for every one of us—if we do it ourselves.

Some Things to Think About

- Get a pad of paper and start thinking about your personal frontier. The right kind of goal is something that takes longer than a week or two to accomplish. It is, however, something realistic enough for you to move a little closer to it every single day. Once you get your goal in writing, read it to yourself every day.

- Spend as much time as you can with other optimistic strivers, as opposed to people who love to dwell on their problems. I can't tell you how many times I've left a convention room or cocktail lounge where a group of salespeople were swapping stories about how bad business is. Optimism and pessimism are both infectious—which would you rather catch?

- Concentrate on being successful first and famous second. Ego almost always gets in the way of ambition. You'll find that the deep personal satisfaction you experience from reaching your goals is far more enjoyable and longer lasting than the fleeting pleasure of being recognized in a restaurant or seeing your name in the papers.

Don't Marry Your Product or Idea
Learn to Leave the Table After Love Stops Being Served

> Drive thy business, or it will drive thee.
> —Benjamin Franklin

Like most Americans of my generation, I was raised to believe that loyalty was one of the most important of all virtues. My father set an example by establishing business relationships that lasted decades; by returning honesty with honesty, respect with respect, and fairness with fairness. I've always tried to meet his standards of loyalty in my own business dealings for two reasons:

- In my personal value system, friendship ranks higher than profits and always will. I simply could not sleep at night if I betrayed someone else's loyalty.
- I have found that long-term relationships are crucial to long-term success. The sharks may gorge themselves for a while, but eventually other sharks come along to feed on *them.*

My philosophy couldn't be more different from the "business as war" attitude that permeated the worlds of business and finance in the 1980s. Within the bounds of fiscal prudence (don't try to sell me a bridge or penny gold stocks), I always try to build relationships on the basis of trust first, rather than starting with an attitude of distrust. It's paid off for me more often than not.

I'll give you an example. A small gift shop in a New England resort community had a very bad summer season, and by fall the mother and son who owned the shop owed me a substantial amount of money. After making numerous phone calls and sending several letters, I was about to turn the account over to a collection agency or an attorney. Then the mother offered to send me a series of checks to settle the account—postdated for the next summer.

Some of my staff thought that accepting checks dated ten to twelve months in the future was too ludicrous even to consider. But I thought that writing the checks was a gesture of good faith that I felt duty-bound to return. Against all logic, I accepted the postdated checks.

I must admit even I was surprised when, the following summer, every single check cleared the bank. I not only collected in full a debt I had written off, but I also enjoyed a tremendous sense of satisfaction. I subsequently offered to ship that gift shop merchandise billed at my cost to help them get back on their feet.

Starting every new relationship with a positive attitude will make a major difference in both your business and personal lives. But there is one extremely important point to remember about loyalty:

> Loyalty is based on a pragmatic relationship that depends on both parties continuing to act in good faith.

In other words, loyalty is like a telephone line that both parties work to keep open. If one party "hangs up" by violating the other's trust, the relationship is ended.

This point is crucial, because I've found a lot of people form business relationships that are a lot like a marriage. Marriage is an emotional commitment made unconditionally "for better or worse, til death do us part." A condition for marriage is falling in love, a process that's not totally rational. I'm old-fashioned, and my lovely wife, Diane, and my two beautiful daughters, Carla and Andrea, are my highest personal priorities. I can't imagine living without them.

However, unconditional emotional commitments are disastrous in business. I've known dozens of very talented people who have been seduced by a product, an idea, a business relationship, even by an unrealistic image of themselves and their abilities. The results range from career frustration to financial catastrophes.

A classic example of the dangers of falling in love was a very talented engineer who invented a new tool for stripping the finish from wood. With the help of a couple friends, he manufactured several dozen of the tools in his basement workshop and peddled them to local hardware stores. The initial supply sold out overnight, and the hardware chains came knocking at his door. He rented a building, hired a work force, and within a year had netted more than $2 million. The inventor bought a big estate, furnished it with expensive European antiques, and began living the lavish lifestyle of a corporate CEO.

Unfortunately, several Asian companies suddenly began flooding the U.S. market with cheaply made copies of the engineer's tool that broke frequently or damaged the wood when used. The price competition slashed the profit margins on the original tool, and consumer complaints about the Asian tools led some retailers to stop ordering completely. Sales and profits plummeted nearly overnight. The inventor could have accepted a lucrative offer for the patent from a major U.S. tool manufacturer with the marketing clout and quality reputation to overcome these problems.

But the inventor loved having his name on the product and his name on the factory. He ignored or fired any employee who urged him to sell his patent. The result: In six months both the company and the inventor were totally bankrupt. He lost his house, his furniture, his automobiles, and, worst of all, the patent for the product he invented. Instead of enjoying a substantial fortune while he applied his considerable technical skills to new inventions, he was absolutely destitute and forced to take a menial job to support his family.

Few stories are this dramatic. But the kind of drastic change in the market for a product or service that afflicted this company is commonplace today. In a world in which even a major superpower like the Soviet Union can disappear in less than a year, every one of us has to be careful to pragmatically reexamine every commitment we have every single day.

I personally learned this lesson shortly after my spectacular success with the *Saturday Night Fever* merchandise. While my wife and I were relaxing in Aruba as guests of the poster licensee, he offered me the chance to distribute the posters for the upcoming movie *Heaven Can Wait*, starring Warren Beatty. The studio was giving this film a big hype too, and Beatty had won the hearts of the female audience with his starring roles in *Bonnie and Clyde* and *Shampoo*. Softened up by a few days on the white sand beaches and a few nights in the casinos, I was quick to take the plunge.

My financial commitment was substantial—hundreds of display units, each housing seventy-two posters. Once again, I sent the marketing material to my sales force. This time, the success of *Saturday Night Fever* led to retailers rushing to get on board what would probably be the next fad. My presales were great. I even did some market research when I gave a speech in a local high school. The students seemed enthusiastic about the movie. I was totally convinced that I was riding yet another big, lucrative wave of consumer demand.

Flushed with confidence, I attended the Boston premiere of the movie with my merchandising manager, Jim Tonner. In the lobby we set up a prominent display of our posters. Then we sat down in the packed theater to watch *Heaven Can Wait*. We thought the film was great, and so did the rest of the audience. Our opinions were shared by the American public, because the movie grossed over $100 million, a huge hit in those days.

As the applause in that Boston theater faded, Jim and I hurried out to the lobby to watch our merchandise being snapped up by the throng of satisfied moviegoers. To our shock and dismay, not one poster was sold. Worse, we didn't even see one person glance at our elaborate display.

As the lobby emptied, my initial emotion could have been anger. I could have railed at the preview audience, complaining that they must have missed seeing the poster display. After all, I had fallen in love with the movie and the merchandise, and my confidence had been reinforced by significant orders from several major retailers in the country. My heart was telling my head that we couldn't be wrong. After all, I stuck with *Saturday Night Fever* when retailers wouldn't touch it with a ten-foot pole and I was rewarded with big profits. I almost persuaded myself that if I ignored these signs and trusted my instincts, I'd win again.

But the rational Stu Taylor wasn't won over. I realized that there was one key difference between the *Saturday Night Fever* posters and the *Heaven Can Wait* posters: In the latter case, it was not retailers but consumers who rejected the merchandise. I couldn't think of a single reason why people who loved the movie didn't love the posters. But I couldn't argue with the fact that not one out of several hundred people would shell out a few bucks to take a souvenir home. Although my heart ached, my head prevailed. I immediately realized that a teenage buying audience could not identify with a middle-aged Warren Beatty. I decided we had a major loser on our hands. Jim and I rushed back to the office to cut our losses.

However, I didn't panic. I also realized that the reputation of my firm could be irrevocably damaged if I protected myself at the expense of my customers. Therefore, I voluntarily canceled all of the orders we had not yet shipped, notifying the salespeople and the retailers involved. Their gratitude was some consolation when I dumped my remaining stock on the carnival and amusement park markets for a fraction of what I had paid for it.

The larger part of the merchandise had already been shipped because of the big presale. I was very happy that I had insisted that these sales be made without consignment, without guarantees, and without any promise of exchange. While many large chains tried to return the merchandise anyway, I refused. I reminded them that they had agreed to take a risk, just as I had. That argument worked.

In the end, I incurred only a modest loss on the *Heaven Can Wait* posters. If I had gone with my emotions, I would have lost much more money and, worse, alienated many customers. I've never forgotten how I felt in the lobby of the theater that night. The problem wasn't that I had been extremely enthusiastic about the merchandise—you'll never sell anything without passion—rather, it was that passion almost overcame reason in the face of hard evidence that my passion was not being returned.

If you are a frequent reader of the business pages, you're familiar with numerous examples of wealthy men and large corporations that stumble because they fall in love with ideas or products. Donald Trump insisted on completing his incredibly expensive Taj Mahal casino despite hard evidence that the Atlantic City gambling revenues were barely supporting existing casinos. The Hunt brothers squandered their multibillion-dollar fortune in a megalomaniacal attempt to corner the world silver market. For years, the American automobile manufacturers refused to change outmoded designs and shoddy quality control procedures even when droves of their former customers were purchasing foreign made cars.

One-sided emotional commitments can be even more damaging to those of us who don't control major corporations or millions of dollars. For example, being a good "company man" is a dangerous, out-moded concept at a time when corporate managements are more ruthless than ever. You *do* owe your employer your maximum effort on the job in exchange for your financial compensation. But you do *not* owe *unconditional* loyalty. Millions of Americans who thought they had jobs for life were devastated when corporate mergers, acquisitions, or downsizing cost them their livelihoods.

Don't let that happen to you. Remain open to opportunities that present themselves outside as well as inside your present company. Weigh those opportunities pragmatically, disregarding any emotional ties you may feel. Remember, your company is not your family.

I can't talk about damaging emotional commitments without discussing the most subtle, but often most crippling, love of all—our erroneous beliefs about ourselves. For example, I know of a man who is a genius with computers. However, he was very shy and introverted as a child, and by the time he reached adulthood he had convinced himself that he was not a "people person." Despite his brilliance, he took a series of low-paying jobs doing routine computer programming. His firmly held self-image prevented him from applying for jobs or seeking promotion to positions that required supervising other people. The result was that he became increasingly bitter and frustrated.

His salvation came in a totally unexpected way—his six-year-old son joined a soccer league that was in desperate need of coaches. Although the man had never volunteered for anything in his life, he couldn't say no to his son. It turned out that he loved dealing with the kids, and he threw himself into the role of coach with great enthusiasm. He gained the respect of the parents and other coaches. The next season he found himself named head of the program for six- to seven-year-olds, and the following season he was voted director of the entire town league.

Still, his fiercely held negative opinion of himself didn't change until he was passed over for yet another promotion. This time his wife confronted him and insisted that he seek counseling. His wife's encouragement and some professional help finally led him to pursue a managerial position with another company. He found, to his surprise, that he was very good at supervising people on the job and communicating with other people. In less than ten years, he became a senior vice president with a Fortune 500 company.

Unfortunately, most people who have unrealistic self-loves or self-hates are crippled for their entire lives. The only way to break away is to ruthlessly examine your emotions, discarding any commitments that aren't positive and pragmatic. What's important is what works today, not what happened yesterday or a year ago. Remind yourself that love is for your personal life—don't get married at work.

Some Things to Think About

- Buy a Gregg-ruled stenographer's notebook, one of those 6″ x 9″ books with a line down the middle of every page. Whenever you're faced with a significant decision, write the pragmatic reasons for each option on opposite sides of the page. Ruthlessly cross out any reasons that involve loyalty you aren't absolutely positive will be returned.

- Save your daily to-do lists and go over them once a month. Jot down the activities that turned out to be a waste of time or that produced negative results. Search for any pattern that is tied to an emotional commitment that is not paying off.

- Don't be reluctant to discuss major decisions with friends or family members who can be impartial. If you feel uncomfortable bringing up subjects like making a career change, make an appointment with a professional job counselor or a psychologist. The cost will be far outweighed by the benefits.

Time Isn't Money
If You Don't Spend It Today, It's Gone Forever

Time is a circus always packing up and moving away.
—Ben Hecht

Early in this century, Albert Einstein shattered one of mankind's most fiercely held beliefs by positing that time wasn't an absolute, fixed quantity. Rather, Einstein's famous Theory of Relativity stated that time was a variable interdependent with speed and mass. For example, time slowed down as speed increased and even came to a halt at the speed of light.

What does this theory about the universe have to do with our everyday lives on a planet where an hour on the parking meter always has exactly sixty minutes? Simply this: Although the measure of time is absolute, its value is relative. In business, I've learned through long experience that an hour today is often priceless compared with the value of an hour tomorrow.

Let me explain. You may receive information that a certain horse is so fit and so fast that it is an absolute lock to win its next race at Santa Anita. That information could be worth a fortune if the race is this afternoon. But it is absolutely worthless if you can't place your bet today. Once a moment in time has passed, it is irretrievable, useless, gone forever.

I believe that most businesses and most businesspeople never approach their true potential in part because the idea that "time is money" has been so thoroughly drummed into their heads. Nearly every day I receive a pitch for a book, seminar, product, or service that promises to save me hours a week that add up to days a year. It's nearly impossible to resist forming the mental image of all those hours piling up in a bank vault to be drawn upon when

39

needed. So, when we're placed with a new demand on our time, we often give into the temptation to say "I'll do it later, when I have more time," for the same reason we often say, "I'll buy that new suit next month when I've saved up the money."

But time is not money. It can be your ally or your enemy. Of course, being efficient is more profitable than being inefficient (I'll discuss working efficiently later in this book), but confusing efficiency with effectiveness is incredibly destructive. Effectiveness is the realization that the only proper use of time is doing today what is important today. Once today is gone, no time-management system, consultant, or tool can bring it back.

Choosing effectiveness over efficiency is difficult because we become addicted to schedules and routines. Because your appointment book is filled today, you probably find yourself saying, "I'll call that potential new customer next week" or "I'll stop by the showroom to see that new product at the trade show next month." If you're like many people, you never get to these calls, so you're never fully aware of the extent of the opportunities you've missed.

My appreciation for the importance of doing important things today began when I started selling plaques out of the trunk of my car. As I said before, I got into the habit of keeping score every day by totaling my sales, subtracting costs, and calculating a net profit. My goal every day was not sticking to my preplanned schedule or routine, but rather boosting that net profit figure. I got used to following up new leads immediately and moving heaven and earth to deliver goods to a customer today, rather than tomorrow. Acting quickly became a habit for me, just as procrastination or undue caution has become a habit for many others.

This habit was largely responsible for my success in the fad business. Webster's dictionary defines a fad as "a practice or interest followed for a time with exaggerated zeal." The business attracted me because "exaggerated zeal" was an excellent description of my business style. If you've ever tried to sell a product that nobody seems to want, you'll appreciate the attractiveness of dealing in products for which people are clamoring.

And what is a fad product? There are four requirements a product must meet before I consider it a fad:

1. Demand for the product must be overwhelming and must always exceed supply.
2. The product must appeal to a large segment of the population.
3. The concept of the product must be understood within just a few seconds.
4. The product more than likely has little or no practical value.

The first requirement means that the key to profiting from a fad is having product to ship today. Timing and aggressiveness are crucial. If you jump in before demand is established, you'll find your warehouse full of fads that never were. On the other hand, a delay of days, even hours, could mean being totally shut out.

The second requirement, by definition, is what makes a fad what it is. The third requirement means that anything too complicated to grasp immediately will fail to engage the short attention span of most people—they will turn their attention quickly to the next matter at hand.

The fourth requirement means a fad is something people want but don't really need—if it weren't, then milk and meat would be fads in what used to be the Soviet Union. When that want is satisfied or disappears, the market for the product disappears. If you don't make a sale and collect the payment today, the market may literally be gone by tomorrow.

Of all of the fads that I've been involved in, the one that most closely fits this classic definition is designer shoelaces. My reactions to this fad are also a classic example of the value of acting today, not tomorrow.

The story begins on the first day of the National Stationery Show held at the old New York City Coliseum in May 1981. I had just opened my display booth when a customer told me about a mob scene on the other side of the first floor. Since I had found buyers to be a pretty cautious and blasé group, I thought the customer was exaggerating. But after three more people passed along the same report, I decided to investigate.

I couldn't believe my eyes. An entire aisle of the convention hall was clogged with hundreds of buyers pushing and shoving in a frantic attempt to get into one specific booth—Lucy's Laces. In this booth, an aggressive young woman was displaying shoelaces printed with all kinds of designs—strawberries, hearts, stars, alligators, pigs, the alphabet, ducks, rocking horses, numbers, and many more. In more than a decade of attending trade shows, I had never before experienced the kind of demand generated by this new product.

It was obvious that the reason for the frenzy was that the demand far exceeded the product Lucy was currently able to supply. At that moment, I had to decide between two courses of action. First, I could join the mob and compete for some of Lucy's laces to distribute. But even if that were possible, I never would have had the profit margin to work with. Or I could go into the shoelace business and produce my own product.

I knew that the second alternative was my only choice. I also knew that lot of much larger companies would have the same idea. As a "little guy" my sole advantage would be acting quickly. If I was to grab a substantial piece of the pie I had to begin not the next day or the next week, but in the next hour.

I did just that. The first thing I ascertained was that there were no copyright infringements. I headed back to my booth, turned over all responsibility to my staff, and headed for a phone booth. I soon located a directory of every shoelace manufacturer in the United States, a list that I remember was very extensive. I sat down and called every single one to find out which met the following four requirements:

1. The company had laces available.
2. The company had the capability to print on the laces.
3. The company could tip the laces.
4. The company had the capability to ship the laces.

I found only five companies could meet these requirements, and three were already doing business with Lucy. I placed huge orders with all five companies, guaranteeing attractive payment terms and any other concessions necessary to receive quick shipments. By acting immediately, I locked up much of the national supply before my competitors could even schedule meetings to decide whether or not to get into the business.

Having located a source of product, I had another decision to make, and this one revolved around ethics. I had no samples of my product to display at this show. One solution was to display some of Lucy's laces and take orders based on my virtually identical products. The second was to display all-white laces along with a list of the designs that were to be printed on them.

The first choice would have been easier and more effective—people like to buy what they see. But I was competing with Lucy, not physically taking her product. I had long ago made the decision not to enter any ethical gray areas, no matter how convenient such a choice would be. So I opted to display the plain white laces.

As it turned out, the demand for the products was so great that it didn't matter. I and the other five members of my staff took orders as fast as we could write. The pressure to deliver those orders was excruciating. The crunch was complicated by the fact that the shoelaces arrived packaged thirty dozen of one pattern to a box. We had to pair up the laces so that they could be sold as a package. This work kept us going until late every night, sometimes all night, seven days a week.

One particularly difficult time occurred on a Tuesday afternoon at the New York Gift Show. The buyer for House of Cards, a fifty-store chain, came to our booth with a huge order. There was one catch: The laces had to be in his stores the following Monday. The prospect of handling these shipments on top of the other work was daunting. We had virtually no supply in the warehouse, and I knew I would have to push my suppliers to the wall as well as my own staff. But I also realized that the potential for this kind of profit might not exist in a few days, much less in a week or a month. I wrote the order and we got to work. Miraculously, we made on-time deliveries to forty-nine of the fifty stores. Recognizing our effort, House of Cards graciously agreed to take delivery on Wednesday at the fiftieth store. My staff received nice bonuses.

The pace was so frenetic that it took months before I added up orders and realized that we had shipped several million pairs of laces that retailed for $1.50 each. By that point, I considered myself very fortunate to have acted so quickly and secured my profit, because the nature of the market began to change in several ways.

First, quality became increasingly important to one segment of the market. At first, as with most fads, demand was so heavy that buyers would snap up any available product of any quality at any price. As supply began to catch up with demand, many retailers began to demand higher standards for shoelace manufacture, design, and printing. Making sure my suppliers delivered high quality work consumed an increasing part of my time and lowered profits.

Second, laces were being custom printed, which added an entirely new dimension to the product.

Then, as in the case of most fad merchandise, lower-priced merchandise from the Far East began flooding into the American market. Retail prices fell to the point where it was difficult for me to make a decent profit on laces produced domestically.

Finally, designer shoelaces became one of the very few fad products that successfully made the transition to a staple product routinely stocked by stores. Laces became a fashion accessory like scarves and jewelry. Companies introduced fat laces, bow laces, neon laces, glow-in-the-dark laces, scented laces, and other varieties keyed to changing fashion. When the business became a fashion rather than a fad business, I got out.

Looking back, the entire experience permanently solidified in my mind the incredible importance of acting today instead of tomorrow. I don't advocate acting rashly—I jumped in only because I knew there was overwhelming demand and because I had the sales and distribution facilities to obtain and process orders. But I did realize from the first instance that I had a very limited window of time in which to make a decision. I jumped at the opportunity, even though it totally disrupted every planned activity of myself and my staff. I could have saved myself a lot of time and effort by moving slowly—imagine sitting down and making 120 telephone calls in less than twenty-four hours. But that time saved would have meant money lost, not gained.

This different perspective on time is one reason that the Japanese have seized control of so many important industries. As you probably have noticed, most important technological breakthroughs in such fields as consumer electronics and computers have been made by researchers in America and other Western nations. The Japanese and other nations in the Far East are often in the position I was in when I discovered the demand for Lucy's Laces—they have to move quickly and decisively or get shut out of the market. While American manufacturers are still doing feasibility studies and holding endless meetings, the foreign competition is in production.

Overseas competitors also understand that every new product will become obsolete far sooner than anticipated. Every employee from the president to the assembly-line worker operates with the knowledge that a day of lost sales can never be recovered. Because they operate with a sense of urgency lacking in many American companies, they have taken much of our market share in many industries.

If you want to attain your personal goals in business and in life, you have to concentrate less on managing time and more on managing yourself. The only place for rigid timetables and schedules is airports, train stations, and other transportation terminals. Appointment books and to-do lists are tools, not mandates. If you have the discipline and courage to change priorities as situations dictate, you'll constantly find yourself in the lead.

My habit of making the most of today was my most important asset in making the transition from the fad business to broadcasting. As a talk show host, I have to live in the present. When a blockbuster baseball trade is announced or another major story breaks, my listeners want to hear about it that night, not the next night or the night after that. I sometimes have to cancel scheduled interviews and scramble to find new guests as late as a half hour before I was due to go on the air. If I don't and if my show doesn't satisfy my audience's need for information, they'll twist the dial and I may never get them back. So I have to treat the show I'm doing today as the most important show I've ever done. That one hour of time is a resource that I can never, ever reclaim.

One useful way to sum up the lessons I've learned is to replace the old saw "time is money" with the new saw "money is time." Instead of picturing the time you save being squirreled away like stacks of bills, picture money eroding as quickly as time. Imagine that you would irretrievably lose sixty dollars an hour if you didn't spend it in the most productive way. If you convince yourself that minutes lost are as valuable as money lost, you'll break old habits and operate most effectively every day.

Some Things to Think About

- Sit down every night and do a mental profit and loss statement for your day. But don't use the number of tasks checked off on your to-do list as an index of success. Rather, evaluate what you didn't do or what you put off for another day. Give yourself negative marks for any opportunities you passed up because you didn't want to change your schedule or embark on a major new task.

• You ease the stress of breaking your routine at work if you consciously avoid being tied to a routine outside the office. Drive to work a different way even if it takes longer, buy your spouse a present for no reason at all, go out to dinner on Wednesday night instead of Saturday night. Flexible, spontaneous people are more open to new opportunities.

• Don't work with a clock in plain sight and try to resist the urge to check your watch frequently. You should learn the concentrate more on what you're doing and less on what time it is.

Business Is a Contact Sport
The Fatter Your Rolodex,
the Fatter Your Wallet

Opportunity is missed by most people because it is dressed in overalls and looks like work.
—Thomas Alva Edison

Of all the types of businesses in the United States, the one that requires management skills most like the fad business is professional sports. In sports, the unpredictability is provided not by fickle consumers, but by events that can suddenly and drastically affect the performance of a team. These events include injuries, slumps, contract disputes, personality conflicts, drug or alcohol problems, and sudden challenges from other teams. The general manager of a sports team must operate with the certain knowledge that a crisis can occur at any time.

How does a general manager cope? By establishing and constantly maintaining a vast information network. A good general manager is in frequent telephone contact with all the other general managers to exchange information and float potential trades. He hires and supervises a network of scouts who constantly evaluate and reevaluate present and potential talent. He stays in touch with agents to head off contract disputes or resolve minor problems. And he constantly travels to meet important executives and scout important players.

The more successful a general manager is at establishing and cultivating a wide network of contacts, the more successful he will be in coping with a crisis by negotiating a quick trade, signing a free agent, promoting a prospect, or making a coaching change. A sports executive who doesn't relish picking up the telephone will not have a job for long.

With our rapidly changing, sometimes chaotic economy introducing unpredictability in almost every industry, every executive and entrepreneur has to operate like the general manager of a sports team. But even though the overwhelming majority of them are sports fans, they don't get the lesson. Business, like football, is a contact sport. The more contacts you have, and the more you enjoy mixing it up with other people, the more successful you'll be.

Establishing, cultivating, and using the widest variety of contacts has played a critical role in my success. Following this principle was the crucial role in my profiting from one of the most explosive fads in the last twenty years—licensed merchandise from the movie *Batman*.

Batman, a "vigilante within the law," made his first appearance in the Detective Comics anthology series in the spring of 1939. He was the brainchild of an eighteen-year-old cartoonist named Bob Kane who had created the character after playing around with images from movies such as *The Mask of Zorro* and *Bat Whispers*. The response to the caped crusader from readers was so positive that *Batman #1* was published in April 1940.

Over the next two decades, Batman became a classic comic character. In the fall of 1966, he burst onto the popular culture scene in a TV series starring Adam West. The show made its debut in a season in which "The Monkees" won the Emmy for outstanding comedy show. Because of the mood of the times, West's Batman was more caricature than character, and his adventures were presented firmly tongue in cheek. The visual style of the show, which featured full-screen WHAMS and POWS interjected into slapstick fight scenes, fit perfectly at a time when tie-dyed shirts were the fashion rage and pop art filled the galleries. The series ended with the 1960s, but it became a cult classic.

In 1978, movie interest in cartoon characters suddenly skyrocketed when *Superman*, starring Christopher Reeve, became a smash box-office hit. Executive producers Benjamin Meiniker and Michael Uslan optioned the movie rights to Batman and took them to the dynamic production team of Jon Peters and Peter Guber. Peters had always been a Batman fan, and he and Guber presented the project to Warner Brothers, which owned DC Comics. The studio was intrigued by the profit potential offered by merchandising from a movie licensed from its own character.

However, as is often the case in the movie business, negotiations dragged on for nearly a decade before a director was finally hired and production was scheduled to begin in September 1988.

Next came one of those odd coincidences that can often trigger a fad. When British television was forced to cancel its live morning talk show because of a strike, they chose to fill its time slot with reruns of the 1960s "Batman" series. To everyone's surprise, the show triggered a "Bat craze" among British teens, who created a large demand for T-shirts and other apparel. As fashion trends tend to do, this interest in Batman crossed the Atlantic, and Batman shirts began to appear on the streets of New York and Los Angeles.

The shirts sold at that time were produced by a few manufacturers who held what we call a "classic" license; that is, a license not related to a specific motion picture or event. Some classic licenses, like those for Disney characters, the Muppets, and Sesame Street characters, produce tens of millions of dollars in sales each year. Others, like Looney Toons, Batman, and Spiderman, produce much smaller sales of merchandise sold primarily in stores where the comic books are purchased.

When Warner Brothers committed to go into production on *Batman*, Licensing Corporation of America, its in-house merchandising division, began negotiating movie-related licenses. Interest was only routine until the spurt in sales of the classic merchandise attracted attention. Competition for movie-related licenses increased, and some manufacturers planned to test small displays of the merchandise at the major annual trade shows in January 1989. I heard about these plans, and I remember making a note to myself to take a special look at these booths at the shows.

A second odd series of events that helped make Batman a phenomenon began when Warner Brothers announced that Michael Keaton had been signed to play Batman. The public's reaction was about the same as if Woody Allen had been signed to play Rambo. The small but extremely vocal contingent of hardcore Batman fans reacted with a barrage of angry letters and telegrams to Warner Brothers and DC Comics. A *Wall Street Journal* article about the controversy made the financial community nervous, and Warner Brothers stock dropped in price.

To counter the negative publicity, Warner hurriedly edited and released a ninety-second trailer for the movie. From its first showing in a Los Angeles movie theater, the trailer became a hit. Small groups of young fans began to line up at theaters, paying six dollars just to see the trailer. Because of all this attention, retailers snapped up the small quantities of Batman merchandise displayed at trade shows. These sales caught my attention. By March of 1989, I realized I had to make a decision about how heavily Taylor Associates would be involved.

We are strictly a distributor of fad merchandise produced by licensees, acting as a middleman between manufacturers and retailers. However, many retailers buy from us for these reasons:

- We are price-competitive.
- We carry top-quality (low end) merchandise and no bootleg items.
- We have merchandise. When demand far exceeds supply, manufacturers don't bother with anything other than very large orders. But even the smallest retailer receives our full attention. However, to get that merchandise, we have to compete with retail giants such as Kmart, Wal-Mart, and Sears, as well as with other distributors and wholesalers.
- We are a one-stop source. A successful movie such as *Batman* may spawn more than a hundred different types of licensed products. Both the quality and saleability of this merchandise varies widely. Our customers have come to depend on us to screen the available products carefully, so they don't have to worry about paying good money for unsaleable junk.

When Batman licenses became hot, we screened many product categories before we decided to carry the following types of products:

T-shirts	earrings, pins, and other
baseball jerseys	fashion accessories
sweatshirts	shoelaces
satin jackets	sterling silver
hats of all types	squeeze bottles
posters	frisbees
marquee posters	postcards
buttons	8″ × 10″ photographs
door hangers	mylar balloons

Our range of merchandise and screening procedures even

attracts busy buyers for large chains, who would often rather make one phone call to us than twenty to different manufacturers.

- We ship faster and offer personalized service. We know a retailer can't make money if the shelves are empty, so we kill ourselves to ship the same day an order is received. More important, we get to know our customers. I touch base with our present and potential accounts on a very regular basis, even if I have nothing special to sell.

Obtaining sufficient quantities of product to sell is the most difficult first step. I can always assure myself of merchandise by committing early, but I risk being stuck with a warehouse full of unsaleable goods if the market never develops—I know people who would trade you a whole truckload of *Days of Thunder* merchandise for a hot meal. On the other hand, if I wait until consumer demand is overwhelming, my competitors will have snatched up all the merchandise, leaving me nothing to distribute.

I don't like gambling. So my only recourse has been to work my very large network of contacts in every area of my business all over the country. This network insures that I hear almost immediately if licensing interest picks up, if a movie-related item sells well at a gift show, or if a major chain makes a significant merchandise commitment. In early 1989 I was constantly on the telephone to retailers, licensees, manufacturer's representatives, and media contacts to glean evidence that the *Batman* hype would actually turn into a marketable fad. Even the intense prerelease hype and publicity generated by *Batman* by no means guaranteed that the movie would generate significant merchandise sales.

One year after I agonized over *Batman*, I had to make a similar decision about *Dick Tracy*. An unprecedented marketing campaign by Disney had led to huge prerelease sales of merchandise to major retailers. I had to make the commitment to purchase a minimum of $200,000 in T-shirts or risk being cut out altogether. I decided to pass. Although I had a great presell on other *Dick Tracy* merchandise, the lukewarm overall merchandising response to the movie would have meant that most of those T-shirts would either have still been in my warehouse or be on sale at some liquidation outlet for $1.97 apiece.

As I made my telephone calls, I came to one important conclusion: The interest in *Batman* was generated by retailers, rather than orchestrated by Warner Brothers. Some felt that the previous summer's hit movie *Who Framed Roger Rabbit* had demonstrated that a movie based on a cartoon figure could attract both child and adult audiences who purchased merchandise to remember it by. Others believed that *Batman* would be successful because Batman was a vigilante crime fighter at a time when nearly everyone was fed up with the inability of law enforcement agencies to stem the tide of drug-related crime and violence. Finally, a few shared my attraction to the powerful, instantly recognizable Batman logo. I saw this logo as an instant Rorschach Test, as I told *Newsweek* magazine, I believed the logo was a symbol of "power, righteousness, invincibility. You don't have to stare at it to get it. It sinks in right away."

One day in early March 1989, after spending twelve hours a day for a week on the phone, I made the decision that *Batman* would be a merchandising phenomenon even if the movie wasn't a critical or commercial success. In retrospect, I realize that I acted in the fifty-ninth minute of the eleventh hour. The fireworks were about to ignite, and if I'd made the decision a few days later, I would have been at the periphery rather than at the center of this huge fad.

Almost all of the similar decisions I've made over the last two decades have also been right. That's why my company is the only national distributor of fad merchandise. Many people in my industry think I'm endowed with special psychic powers, like a guru or seer. It sounds glamorous, but it couldn't be further from the truth. My secret is simple: hard work. I talk to far more people on a far more regular basis than anyone else in my line of work. I've expended a lot of effort making sure that I have as wide a range of contacts as possible. I not only keep in touch with corporate presidents and important buyers, but also with the owners of small businesses who are dealing with customers over their counters every single day.

My system for making and keeping contacts is simple. Over the years, I've found trade shows, conventions, meetings, receptions, and other social events to be the best place to meet people. Before I go anywhere that I'm going to meet people, I thoroughly prepare myself. I find out how to dress—if I'm in doubt, I've found it's always better to overdress. I make sure I have a pen and a notepad to jot down names, addresses, telephone numbers, and other information. Finally, I prepare myself mentally to assert my presence by looking informed, relaxed, and in control.

When I enter a room, I begin to circulate immediately. Since my primary reason for attending the event is to meet people, I stay away from the food and the bar. If I'm hungry, I eat ahead of time. I approach people with a big smile, introduce myself, and begin some pleasant small talk. I stay away from excessive humor because it's risky—if the joke bombs, you look terrible. Instead, I ask questions about the person's business and family. I always show my interest by making sure I maintain eye contact and by answering directly any questions asked of me. I don't spend too much time with any one person and I try not to get isolated in a corner of the room. Finally, I end every conversation by exchanging business cards or making notes on my pad.

After the event is over, I try to go over the business cards and notes to make sure I don't forget anything important. I immediately follow through on any specific action that came up in conversation—for example, sending out price lists of my merchandise or scheduling an appointment to see someone else's products. Even if nothing specific came up in conversation, I try to follow up with a brief telephone call or letter to say that I enjoyed meeting the person and hope to keep in contact in the future.

All the business cards and names go into my Rolodex. I work that Rolodex whenever I have a spare couple of minutes in the day. I make sure that I keep in contact with people even when there's no pressing reason to do so. I can't tell you how many times a manufacturer of a hot fad product has filled my orders first because I took the time to keep in touch when he had nothing I urgently needed. Because I'm thorough and courteous, I've developed excellent relationships even with people others consider impossible to deal with.

If you want to be a success in any field, you've got to be a people person with the widest possible range of contacts. I'm absolutely astounded by executives who only contact people when they need something. Making people feel used builds hostility and resentment. The more people who like you, the easier it will be to do business.

Some Things to Think About

- Maintain and groom your Rolodex as if it were the garden in front of your home. Use the back of each card for a few personal notes about the person on the front—name of spouse, names and ages of children, special interests, etc.

- Get into the habit of contacting three people a day who you have no specific reason to call or write. At the end of the year you will have made 750 additional personal contacts.

- Practice your people skills every chance you get. Use the same techniques at purely social events such as cocktail parties so that they'll be second nature when you attend business gatherings.

Be a Person of Character

*The Only Lie That Will Ever
Net You a Dollar Is the Lie
You Didn't Tell*

A commentary on the times is that the word *honesty* is now
proceeded by *old fashioned*.

—Larry Wolters

After reading the business pages in the go-go 1980s, I often felt
as out of date as spittoons and the twenty-five-cent haircut. The
credo embraced by the business community was echoed perfectly
by the Michael Douglas character in the movie *Wall Street*: "Greed
is good." Financial manipulators like Michael Milken and Ivan
Boesky bent and broke the law to rake in hundreds of millions of
dollars peddling junk bonds. Hordes of wheeler-dealers and con
men swarmed around the nation's savings and loans, feeding on
the hard-earned deposits made by ordinary working people. Financial raiders such as Carl Icahn purchased huge stakes in
corporations that gave them leverage to demand huge payments
known as greenmail to leave the corporations alone. Encouraged
by a laissez-faire attitude of the times, the rich got fabulously
richer year by year throughout the decade.

I'm hardly opposed to making money. But I found the prevail-
ing attitude of the 1980s repugnant. More to the point, I believe
that unethical business tactics are profoundly counterproductive
in the long run. For example, look at the legacy left us by the
"robber barons" of the last decade: Milken, Boesky, and many
others received jail terms and paid huge fines; we taxpayers are
paying hundreds of billions of dollars to bail out savings and loan
depositors; junk bonds and leveraged debt destroyed many cor-

porations, which resulted in financial losses for investors and job losses for employees. I believe that the recent deep recession was primarily caused by a moral, rather than fiscal, crisis. Individual greed sapped our financial resources, making it more difficult to compete with foreign corporations.

You and I may not run Fortune 500 companies or control hundreds of millions of dollars in assets. But we do start out in our careers with an asset more precious than money: an unblemished reputation. Central to my success in life is the fact that I have made preserving that reputation the top priority when making every business decision. To me, "doing the right thing" means doing so ethically as well as financially. Not only do I sleep better at night, but I have also proved that Leo Doroucher was dead wrong when he said, "Nice guys finish last."

I was introduced to "old fashioned honesty" by my father. He conducted his business according to two very simple tenets:

- Always do what you say you're going to do.
- If you can't, explain promptly and truthfully.

As a buyer and seller of distressed and surplus merchandise, my father knew he'd never again see many of the people he did business with. He also had many opportunities to make much needed extra money by reneging on a verbal commitment to sell to one buyer when a better offer came along. But Bert Taylor treated everyone the same and never cut a corner. He was honest, reliable, and paid every invoice he ever received on the same day he received it. Some other people in his business called him a sucker for passing up an easy buck. Yet as the years passed, Bert's reputation became a more and more important asset. Sellers and buyers sought him out because they knew he could be trusted completely. He prospered for decades while most of the people who snickered at his ethics went bankrupt.

From my first day in business, I've rigidly adhered to my father's tenets. After more than twenty years, my reputation has become a formidable business tool. A perfect example of its value is the crucial role it played after I made the decision to devote all my resources to selling merchandise from the move *Batman*.

Deciding to participate in a fad is one thing; obtaining merchandise to sell is another. Within hours of my decision to sell *Batman* merchandise, I had compiled a complete listing of the approximately one hundred Batman licensees who were producing approximately three hundred different products. I weeded out the products I wasn't interested in, then ordered the remaining items in order of importance to me.

In today's fad market, T-shirts are the cornerstone of any product line. I knew that by the time the T-shirt licensees reached full capacity, they would have orders for ten times as many shirts as they could ship. Taylor Associates had to be at the head of the line for merchandise, so I handled all the negotiations personally.

I spent almost every minute of the next forty-eight business hours on the telephone. In dealing with the already overwhelmed executives, I relied on carefully developed techniques I call the five C's. Two of them I have discussed previously:

- *Contacts*: Most people I called knew me or knew of me. The hard work I'd put in developing and maintaining relationships pays off when a fad is raging.
- *Capacity*: I knew *Batman* T-shirt suppliers would be imposing minimum orders of one hundred dozen at a cost of four thousand dollars for each of four to six different designs. That minimum of twenty to thirty thousand dollars was beyond the capacity of all but the largest retailers, but was no problem for me.

  As important as these two factors were, they still didn't give me a clear advantage. Sears, Kmart, Wal-Mart, and other large chains easily matched me in purchasing power, and many buyers and distributors had a wide range of contacts. To be first in line, I had to use the following additional weapons.

- *Courtesy*: No matter how harried or stressed I am, I've trained myself to be patient, sympathetic, and friendly to everybody from receptionist to chief executive. It works wonders.
- *Character*: When a fad is hot, licensees hear from every fly-by-night operator in the business. And large retail chains are notorious for placing large orders, then canceling or refusing some of the merchandise at the last minute. I insisted that licensees who didn't know me personally call respected industry figures who did. My reputation for

honesty, for doing exactly what I said I'd do when I said
I'd do it, was especially important to executives working
under excruciating pressure.

• *Cash*: When it comes to money, I'm a fiscal Neanderthal.
Like my father, I abhor debt. I pay all my bills on time
and I always take the 2 percent discount offered for quick
payment. As a result, I have an impeccable credit rating
and an ample cash reserve.

When I'm competing for merchandise, I offer to let
suppliers check my credit by telephone to save time. Then,
to sweeten the pot, I authorize suppliers to send the first
shipment C.O.D. Because cash flow is so crucial to a
manufacturer struggling to keep up with demand, instant
payment for a large order is nearly always irresistible. My
offer to pay upon receipt also establishes an atmosphere of
trust.

In my conversations with licensees, I discovered that the demand
for *Batman* merchandise was even more intense than I had expected. But product by product, I managed to lock in supplies.
My reputation was the critical factor.

The reputation of my firm was also crucial in the second part
of the process of profiting from a fad—selling to retailers. Because speed is of the essence, I rarely bother with sophisticated
catalogs or fancy sales material unless they are provided by the
manufacturer. Remember Principle #5: Time Isn't Money. As
soon as we locked in a product, we faxed a description and prices
to our network of more than 220 sales representatives all over the
country. At the same time, we used faxes, mail, and telephone
calls to blitz major customers. Retailers were clamoring for *Batman* merchandise, and before they placed an order, they wanted
to be sure the merchandise would be delivered as promised. My
long record of reliability resulted in an increasing tide of orders.

In less than a week, we had received and shipped our first
order. I vividly remember the details. The merchandise went to
Retail Mall Concepts, a Michigan-based firm that operates a chain
of stores called What's New. The owner of the company, an astute
businessman after my own heart, had responded to my enthusiasm by sending payment in advance so he'd get the first shipment.
He never even asked for terms of payment. Two days later we
received a call telling us that the entire shipment blew out of the

stores. Literally, a cheer went up in our office. We were off and running.

We were soon working seventeen to eighteen hours a day, seven days a week. On a typical day, I would arrive at the office shortly after dawn to find delivery trucks lined up on the street. The merchandise on those trucks overflowed our warehouse, filling up all the corridors in our office as well as our large fenced-in parking lot. The demand for that merchandise was so great that some retailers showed up in person with cash in hand, some from as far away as Denver. The telephones never stopped ringing and the fax machines spit out order after order twenty-four hours a day. Those orders had to be logged, credit checks had to be run, payment terms verified, invoices issued, shipping manifests prepared, and the order picked and packed for shipment.

I had an incredible staff, most of whom had been with me for more than a decade. Every single person understood that in the fad business there's no guarantee that what's in demand today will be in demand tomorrow. That's why we set a goal of processing all paperwork and shipping out all merchandise on the day on which it was received. Because my staff was as proud of our reputation as I was, we almost invariably met that goal. At the height of the *Batman* fad, we shipped more than five hundred orders each day.

As the June 23, 1989, opening of the movie approached, the demand for merchandise reached its peak. To insure a maximum supply, I discarded a lot of the standard procedures of doing business. Even though most suppliers were weeks behind on their invoicing, I started sending them checks for as much as twenty thousand dollars as frequently as three times a week, to make sure I stayed at the head of the line for goods. I told my staff to okay any shipping premiums or special handling charges to get merchandise in the door today rather than tomorrow. I also agreed to accept any increase in minimum orders or other extraordinary stipulations placed by manufacturers.

However, no matter how many unfilled orders we had, I refused to bend on quality standards. We inspected each shipment carefully, and used the same criteria to reject inferior *Batman* merchandise as we did in rejecting less popular merchandise. Our reputation has always been more important than a few extra dollars. For that same reason, we absolutely refused to purchase any of the unlicensed, or black market, *Batman* material that flooded into the country.

By August, Batmania was in its sixth month. *Batman* had not only been a box office success, but had spawned the most successful sale of movie-related merchandise since *Star Wars*. Just how big the fad had been for my company came home to me one day when I added up a few columns and discovered exactly how much merchandise we had shipped. I reflected that if I hadn't had extraordinary advantages in dealing with suppliers, we wouldn't have gotten our hands on one-tenth that amount.

At the same time as I enjoyed the success, I was faced with another difficult task—deciding when to stop ordering merchandise. I knew from my experience with *Saturday Night Fever* and many other movies that consumer demand can literally disappear overnight. When that happens, retailers will refuse to accept ordered merchandise when the truck arrives and many will ship back cartons that suddenly have become designated as "damaged" goods. This leaves distributors like myself with a warehouse full of virtually worthless merchandise, wiping out months of profit. To protect themselves, some distributors use the same tactics as retailers. But at Taylor Associates we have always honored our orders and refused to lie about the condition of merchandise to save ourselves some money. Once again, the potential long-term damage to our reputation outweighs the short-term benefits. Pulling the plug too early, on the other hand, also disrupts relationships with suppliers, angers retailers who can't get product, and costs lost profits.

After months of eighteen-hour days, I feared my exhaustion would affect my judgment. I decided to go ahead with a family vacation to Nantucket. Every day, I'd get up early, check in with my staff, then work my network of contacts on the East Coast for an hour or two before heading to the beach. By three in the afternoon, I'd head back to our rented house to spend another couple of hours with contacts on the West Coast. As Friday arrived, I had heard that a handful of retailers in the New York and Los Angeles metropolitan areas had curtailed or stopped their ordering of new *Batman* merchandise. I also noted that I was seeing less and less of the *Batman* logo in retail newspaper ads. At the same time, the plethora of *Batman* shirts on the beach convinced me that the market had been saturated.

On Friday afternoon, I took a deep breath, then called the office. I stopped all new orders and directed an intensified sales effort to clear out the warehouse. For the second time, my timing was nearly perfect. Except for some earrings and other fashion accessories I felt duty bound to accept even though they arrived late, we got out nearly clean. I learned later that many other companies that had been key participants in the fad hadn't been so lucky. Among the casualties was the T-shirt company to which I had sent so many checks as payment in advance.

Among the chief lessons to be learned from this story is that a life-long practice of honoring commitments will reap rich rewards. Good character is one of the most powerful and least appreciated tools of the businessperson. It also takes a lifetime to build, but can disappear overnight.

Of the many other examples I can cite to illustrate this, the one that sticks most in my mind involves the eastern region of a nationwide truck-leasing company. For more than a decade, this region had been run by a man who used his position to embezzle money. Corruption seeped down, until every local office manager was taking kickbacks from suppliers, overbilling customers, cheating on expense accounts, conspiring to steal parts and supplies, and was involved in a host of other illegal activities. Corporate headquarters finally woke to the scandal when customers began fleeing in droves. Teams of highly paid and highly educated managers failed to stem the tide or clean up the mess. When a new president was hired, auditors recommended that the entire region be dissolved.

However, the new president reached out and hired the most unlikely of candidates as regional manager. This man, I'll call him Tony, had no education beyond high school and couldn't pound out a profit and loss projection, much less a sophisticated financial analysis, to save his life. Although he had been a terminal manager for a large freight company, he had no truck-leasing experience. His salary in his former position was less than one-third of what the ex-regional manager had been paid. However, Tony had two assets that the new corporate president valued—he was blunt and he was totally honest. In his interview, Tony told the president, "I never lie. I have so much trouble remembering what I'm supposed to do that I couldn't possibly remember what I'd said I'd do but didn't."

Tony's hiring turned out to be a brilliant move. He tackled every problem and complaint head on, using brutal honesty and hard work as his only sales technique. Within a year, he'd not only convinced present and former customers that he was more reliable than previous management, he'd convinced them that he was more reliable than the management of competitors. In less than three years, he took his region from multimillion dollar annual losses to being the most profitable region in the country. In the process, he earned huge bonuses for himself.

Even if you don't have a cent of capital to invest in a new business, you have the potential to use the asset that Tony and I have used so effectively. Being an ethical businessperson doesn't mean that you can't be tough or hard driving. But it does mean that you should become a fanatic about keeping any promises that you make and about honestly and forthrightly admitting to the inevitable problems that will occur.

Some Things to Think About

- The best way to avoid breaking a lot of promises is to avoid making rash promises in the first place. In one-on-one relationships we always want to say what people want to hear. It takes discipline to resist the temptation to make a promise that you know you can't keep.

- Write down any commitments you make, no matter how trivial. If you promise to call someone at 10:00 A.M. on Thursday, make sure you pick up the phone exactly on time. Keeping promises is like quitting smoking—you'll often be tempted, but you have to be fanatic about resisting. One or two, and you're addicted again.

- Associate with trustworthy people. You'll be much more likely to give in to the temptation to cut corners if you socialize with people who routinely do the same thing. One major slip can affect your reputation for years.

Silence Is Golden
You'll Never Learn Anything While Your Lips Are Moving

> To say the right thing at the right time,
> keep still most of the time.
> —John Roper

Mel, a good customer who's also a good friend, called me some time ago, and in the course of the conversation he asked about my new sports talk show. After less than a year hosting a Tuesday late-night hour and filling in on weekends, I had recently been named host of a prime-time hour heard five nights a week on more than two hundred stations. I took over from Bill Buckner, the former baseball all-star who quit to take a hitting instructor's job in the Toronto Blue Jays organization. Booking guests for five nights was a lot more work than booking guests for one, and that afternoon I'd spent hours fruitlessly trying to track down a major sports celebrity I wanted for my show that evening.

I guess some of the frustration came out in the conversation, because Mel said, "Stu, tell me what other guests you've booked this week."

I replied, "So far I've got Julius Erving, the famous Dr. J., tomorrow night. George Foreman is coming on Wednesday. And Baseball Hall of Fame legend Bob Feller will be on at the end of the week."

Mel said, "My brother has been a broadcaster for more than ten years, and he'd give anything to interview just one of those guys. Lighten up, Stu."

I had to admit he was right. "I guess I've been lucky," I said.

"Luck has nothing to do with it," my friend replied. "With your gift of gab, you're a natural."

I thanked him for the kind words, then went back to work. That evening, while driving to the studio, I was listening to a cassette of one of my recent shows. I review every show at least twice, a habit that's paid rich dividends. I had been particularly happy with this show the first time I'd heard it, and now I thought to myself, "Stu, Mel is right. You do have some natural talent."

But as the tape played I also realized that my friend had been only partially correct about where my talents lay. After decades of selling, I was an effective talker. But so were a million other salespeople who wouldn't last a day on the radio. My special talent, such as it is: I am a very good listener.

From my first show, I understood that my audience tuned in to hear Julius Erving talk about basketball, not Stu Taylor. My job was to concentrate fully and intensely on what my guest was saying instead of thinking about what I was going to say next. By listening, I could be responsive, asking the right questions, jumping in with a comment, or changing the subject if the interview started to drag. Invariably, when my show was over, the guest would tell me how much he or she enjoyed the interview and comment about how comfortable he or she felt. A comfortable guest makes for good radio.

You may be surprised that I emphasize listening as a talent. If we surveyed any twenty people at random, odds are nineteen would describe themselves as good listeners. That's because they think of listening as "not talking." But listening is an active pursuit that requires discipline and hard work. If that sounds strange to you, sit in on a one hour lecture and take detailed notes. I guarantee you'll walk out exhausted.

Academic demands make us better listeners in school, but most of us soon lose those skills when we go out to the working world. Fortunately, I had an experience in my senior year of college that indelibly fixed the importance of listening in my mind.

As I've mentioned before, I majored in experimental psychology at Northeastern University, which had a terrific cooperative education program. My cooperative work setting in my senior year was with Teaching Systems, Inc., where I was assigned to develop a set of sales training manuals for Volkswagen of America. To research the project, I traveled extensively throughout the eastern United States to interview the top VW salespeople about their techniques.

This assignment introduced me to a fascinating world. As a hot-shot psychology major, I expected that these men would list a few simplistic techniques that I'd have to dress up with the psychological principles I'd learned. I couldn't have been more wrong. These salespeople had insights into the psychology of buying and selling that put some of my professors to shame. Their techniques were both sophisticated and subtle. Instead of spending the interviews glancing at my watch, I hated to see them end.

Of all the things I learned, the most memorable was the importance of *qualifying a prospect*. The phrase is familiar to all salespeople. But most of them believe that the process merely requires finding out if a prospect is serious about making a purchase and has the resources available to do so. That's why most salespeople stop listening when the best salespeople are just starting.

A typical example of the superficial techniques of many salespeople occurred a couple years ago when a writer friend of mine decided to upgrade his computer system from the rather primitive model he'd been using for years. He didn't have a lot of technical knowledge about computers, so he very sensibly typed a detailed description of the tasks for which he needed an upgraded system. He also listed his price range and the make and model of the printer with which his new computer would be linked.

He knew he could save money by buying from a mail-order company, but he wanted the input of a knowledgeable salesperson. He visited six large computer retailers, five of which were branches of large national chains. He handed each salesperson his written requirements, then sat down for at least half an hour to explain his needs in more detail. The systems and software recommended by all six were remarkably similar, which made him confident he was on the right track. He chose one retailer because of price and location, took his system home, plugged it in, and began to work.

Within a few hours he discovered that not one of the salespeople he talked to had really listened to him. The expensive database program packaged with his new system was designed to handle numbers, not the textual material he normally dealt with. Both the random access memory and the capacity of the hard disk were too small to handle a desktop publishing program that he was contractually obligated to use to produce his next book. He'd even been given the wrong cable to link his computer with his printer. He finally realized that every one of the six salespeople had tried to sell him one of their standard systems. After they'd discovered he was serious about purchasing and had a specific budget in mind, they had stopped listening. His written list of requirements and detailed explanation of his needs had passed over their heads.

He returned the system, then called a number of other writers for advice until he had a list of the hardware and software he really needed. Then he called a mail-order company, saving himself more than 30 percent. That's why he's not surprised today when several of the large retail computer chains have declared bankruptcy while the mail-order companies are flourishing.

This story is typical because salespeople are trained primarily to talk. They can quote reams of information about their products and can immediately quote the correct response to each typical sales objection. But they tend to listen like a radio tuned to a narrow channel. They only hear that the customer wants to buy and has money to spend. They're deaf to the detailed needs expressed by the customer, as well as to the subtle nuances of facial expression and body language that often mean as much as words.

When I started in business for myself, listening well enough to truly qualify prospects wasn't just a technique, but a matter of survival. Because I was paying every cent of expenses out of my own pocket, I couldn't afford to waste a single call. On the very first call I had to find out as much as possible about each store owner I spoke with; what kinds of merchandise did he sell, what was his sales volume, how long was his inventory turnover time, when did he like to do his buying, when did he pay his bills, and a lot more. I also had to hone my ability to read between the lines to determine exactly how interested a merchant really was.

Qualifying a customer was easier when I had just one product line. My experience increased with the variety of merchandise I was selling. By the time I became a national fad distributor, I had trained my staff in the sophisticated process of determining and meeting the needs of all of our accounts from the small gift shop to the large national retail chain.

By this time, I spent most of my time on a task that required even more complicated listening skills—determining what trends and fads were about to burst onto the scene. I want to emphasize once again that I'm a fad finder, not a fad maker. Setting out to create a fad from scratch is like trying to catch lightning in a bottle. Literally thousands of new products are submitted for my review every year, and without exception every person who submits a product to me is convinced that it will become the next national rage. Even though the vast majority are poorly made, ill-conceived, or have some other flaw that I know from experience will make them unsuccessful, I listen courteously and carefully to every sales pitch. One reason is that I might be wrong and the product might find a market after all. More frequently, the salesperson or inventor comes up with a more marketable product in the future and will bring it to me first.

When I've eliminated the obvious losers, I still see perhaps a hundred products that are as cleverly conceived as the Slinky, the Pet Rock, or other fad products that have become huge successes. Of these, one or two will have significant sales potential. I have yet to find anyone who can develop a rational system for predicting ahead of time which one of the hundred products will be a winner. I've seldom tried. Instead, I monitor the response when these products reach the market.

I get on the telephone, call people, ask questions, and listen. I listen to the radio, TV news, and to conversations when I'm attending events or even shopping. I make sure to go over the newspapers and major news magazines every week. As I do, I ask myself, "What are people interested in? What are they talking about? Is there anything new I don't understand?"

What I don't do is pay much attention to the self-proclaimed trend spotters or futurists from Alvin Toffler and John Naisbitt to Faith Popcorn. I've found that these people tend to make a prediction first, then marshal evidence to support the prediction. In other words, they embrace any facts that support their beliefs and ignore facts that don't.

Guarding against such selective listening is a difficult task that requires constant attention. A good example took place the summer after *Batman* produced such blockbuster sales and profits. I've already mentioned that Disney's intense promotion of *Dick Tracy* anointed that film as the successor to *Batman*. I certainly wanted to believe the hype—my coffers could use the filling. Major retailers such as JCPenney jumped aboard early, placing huge orders. As I mentioned before, I was tempted to place a large order. But as with *Batman*, I forced myself to work the telephones first to find out how retailers were likely to react.

I didn't like what I heard. The hype for the movie and merchandise seemed to be orchestrated strictly by the studio; small retailers were adopting a cautious, wait-and-see attitude. Some people were worried because kids, who buy a lot of movie-related merchandise, had absolutely no idea who Dick Tracy was. To others, the central image of the movie—Warren Beatty in the fedora and full-length yellow coat—seemed silly. This was in stark contrast to the electrifying image of the *Batman* logo.

Despite the decidedly mixed response I was receiving, I almost caved in to the pressure from the T-shirt licensee and to my own desire to feel the rush of riding another fad. But that would have been my first violation of the commonsense principles that had made me so successful.

Dick Tracy turned out to be a modestly successful movie that generated moderately successful merchandise sales. It was far from a smash, which meant I could get all the T-shirts I wanted without risking a huge initial investment. I made an adequate profit, avoided a much larger loss, and reaffirmed my principle of basing my decisions on what I hear, not on what I want to hear.

Another story that comes to mind when I think about the power of listening involves a company that manufactured high quality furniture for sale through interior designers. The company had encountered an increasing amount of competition, and its salespeople were having trouble even scheduling appointments with the top designers. Then the president of the company had a brainstorm: Instead of trying to tell designers what products they had, why not invite designers to tell the company what products and services they'd like to have? He immediately set to work organizing a tour of twenty-seven major U.S. cities. In each, the twelve most prominent designers were invited to a two-hour breakfast session.

The response was overwhelming. Designers who wouldn't give the company's salespeople ten minutes in their offices were more than happy to spend two hours talking to a company that would listen. The company recorded all the sessions, then sent printed summaries to the participants. The results: a 45 percent increase in sales in the next six months, plus a brand-new reputation as a company that cared.

If you want to sniff out new trends, find out what's really happening in the marketplace, or impress new and prospective customers, the best tool to use is not computers or market research studies. Rather, it's your ears. Compulsive listeners always leap ahead of even the smoothest talkers.

Some Things to Think About

- Record your next meeting or sales call. When you play back the tape, use a stopwatch or a watch with a second hand to add up the percentage of time you're talking instead of listening. If you're talking more than 50 percent of the time, you're not a good listener. Talking one-third of the time or less means that you've used the meeting to educate yourself.

- When you're listening, concentrate on how you can *act* on what you're hearing, not on what you should *say* in response. *Acting* means providing additional information requested by a customer, exploring an interesting new marketing idea, or even typing and circulating a summary of the meeting.

- Take notes—lots of them. The act of taking notes awakens good habits acquired in our school days. After the meeting, review the notes for accuracy, then keep them in a file so you can consult them before a future meeting.

Have No Shame
You'll Never Be a Wallflower if You Don't Wait to Be Asked

Success is a journey, not a destination.
—Ben Sweetland

Maury Simonds has been my very good friend since we met at the Cape Cod gift show more than twenty years ago. Since then Maury has seen me work hundreds of shows. The pace at which I work a show, while controlled, stops just short of frenetic. I move quickly from booth to booth, floor to floor, ferreting out the hot products, then moving in to make deals. Sometimes things happen so quickly that I've been known to jot notes on my hands so I don't forget a contact or the key terms of a deal.

Maury, whose approach to business and life is a lot more laid back than mine, tends to watch me with a bemused look. When I come back from making yet another contact, he often shakes his head and scolds, "Kid, you've got no shame."

Maury's kidding, but he's also right. I pay my bills on time, stay far away from anything unethical, and am always polite and courteous. But within those parameters, I have done and will continue to do anything and everything I can to promote myself and my business. I find absolutely nothing shameful or embarassing about offering to sell something to someone or asking someone if I can purchase their products.

It always strikes me as odd when I'm described as an "aggressive" businessman or a "real go-getter." To me, being aggressive and a go-getter are parts of the definition of businessman. If they aren't, that means that being passive or having a "let-them-come-to-me" attitude is a reasonable way to conduct business. I can't accept that.

Of course, I understand that shyness makes it difficult for a lot of people to be comfortably aggressive in their business dealings. I know, because when I was growing up I had at least the normal allotment of shyness. But I found that shyness was just another obstacle in the way of achieving success, no more difficult to overcome than lack of formal education, lack of family money, or other similar problems. With the proper attitude and lots of hard work, anyone can "have no shame."

I made great strides in overcoming my shyness on my very first job. I always loved amusement parks, and when I turned fifteen, I managed to snag a summer job as a carnival game barker in one of the largest Boston area parks. The park offered a number of the usual games, but the most lucrative was the cigarette/candy game. This booth featured a board painted with colored squares numbered one to eight. Players wagered a dime on one of the squares, then waited while the barker pressed a button that spun a wheel divided into eight segments. Whatever number was lit when the wheel stopped determined which player won. The barker flipped a lever that dumped the coins into a hopper, paid off the winner with a couple of packs of cigarettes or candy, then started taking bets again.

Working the cigarette game was the most prestigious job in the park. Competition for the job, although brutal, was based on a very simple criterion: The barkers who brought in the most money worked the game. From the moment I started I desperately wanted to run that game. However, up to that time I had never been an extrovert. So before I could compete with others I had to wage a war within myself. Was my goal more important than my shyness, or vice versa?

The goal won, hands down. I watched the best barkers, and saw they were doing absolutely nothing embarassing—the games were honest, the prizes were fair. I realized that what was shameful was not doing my job with the maximum energy and enthusiasm I could muster. From then on, when I manned a booth, I was enthusiastic, friendly, funny, even a little crazy. Sure enough, I soon worked my way up to the cigarette game.

I've approached my work with complete energy and enthusiasm ever since. I was giving a speech one day when someone asked me what kind of person I'd look for if I were hiring a replacement for myself. I replied that I'd want someone who believes that the market for his or her products or services is infinite. No matter how successful, this person would always have something to pursue. I would want someone who knows that you have to go out to get business, not wait until it comes to you. This person would share the philosophy of my company: If we have 5,000 accounts, we could have 15,000, 25,000, 100,000 or more.

Pursuing success, whether by its selling a product or service, raising money to start a business, or finding a new job, requires mastering the art of contacting people you don't know. In other words, you have to become an expert in what's commonly called "cold sales." When I started my own business selling out of the trunk of my car, every call I made was a cold call. Almost every major success I've had since then has involved critical telephone contacts with people I'd never met—sales reps when I landed the *Saturday Night Fever* deal, manufacturers when I leaped into designer shoelaces, licensees when *Batman* became a phenomenon. Today, I'm still making important cold calls when I contact sports celebrities to ask them to be guests on my show.

Over the years, I've worked with my employees to help them approach sales calls with the same enthusiasm I have. Basically, they have to overcome two hurdles. The first is fear of rejection. I think this fear has its roots in adolescence, especially in our first experiences dating. The most difficult cold call in the world for a fifteen-year-old boy is picking up the phone and asking for a date. Many girls, on the other hand, are raised to believe that it's "unseemly" to ask at all. Adolescence also has other traumatic social hurdles such as trying out for a sports team, applying to colleges, and seeking acceptance from social cliques. These activities are personally important to teenagers, so rejection wounds deeply.

Business, however, is not personal. And rejection, rather than being the exception, is the rule. Almost everyone who sells anything hears no five, ten, fifteen, even twenty times more often than yes. And when a customer says no to you, the odds are that he or she would also say no to me or to the most gifted salesperson in the world. That's because the customer is choosing not to use the products or services you're offering, not because you're not a good person.

I think all of us could learn a lesson from entertainers in not taking rejection personally. Both of my daughters are gifted singers, dancers, and actresses. I spend a good deal of my time chauffeuring them to auditions for commercials and plays. At these auditions, as with auditions for adult performers, there are often hundreds competing for one part. Final decisions are made not only on the basis of talent, but on arbitrary details of physical appearance—the exact color of hair, a well-placed dimple, a certain kind of smile. My girls have fortunately been chosen for a large number of wonderful roles and assignments. But they've also had to learn that they can't experience the thrill of being chosen in an audition if they can't tolerate the still more frequent experience of watching someone else get chosen. At their young ages, they've learned the valuable lesson that you feel disappointment without experiencing rejection.

If fear of rejection is a problem for you, you should keep this in mind: By and large, the most successful salespeople are those who make the most calls. While technique and experience help, there is no substitute for plain, old-fashioned hard work. And the more contacts you make, the less rejection will bother you.

However, rejection isn't the only reason people don't like making cold calls. The second hurdle most have to overcome is uncertainty about the best procedure to use. Over the years, I've found that the following techniques work best. (I use selling as an example of the purpose of the call. Of course, selling something isn't the only reason you may want to contact people you don't know. You may be looking to purchase a product or services, gather information, explore a new job or career, or acquire funding for a new business or the expansion of your present business.)

- Find out as much as you can about a company before you call, especially anything that provides you with a connection. For example, you may already sell to one of its suppliers or competitors.
- Try to find out who the decision maker is. The receptionist can often provide this information. Before you speak with a person, ask the receptionist or the secretary the correct pronunciation of the person's name and his or her exact title. With this information, you can address the person correctly.
- Identify yourself and your company, and never falsify the intent of your call. Many self-proclaimed experts tell

salespeople that they can "get around" a secretary by pretending they are friends of the boss, by announcing the boss has won a contest, or by falsely claiming a mutual friend. These techniques enrage me—I can't imagine entering into any kind of business agreement with a person who begins our relationship by lying.

- Get to the point immediately. If you don't know the person you're calling, don't ask how they are and don't make small talk. By getting directly to the crux of the matter, you are sending the message that you are a professional who understands the value of time to the person you're calling. However, don't go overboard by asking, "Am I calling at a bad time?" That makes it too easy for the person to say, "Yes."

- Avoid forced-choice questions that lead you to a dead end. For example, don't ask, "Are you interested in purchasing more life insurance?" What if the answer is no? Instead, ask, "Do you carry life insurance?" Then if the answer is no you can follow up the question by explaining why life insurance should be carried. Establish a rapport by talking about a person's needs before asking for an order.

- Talk about features and benefits together. But don't belabor any points. You should be sensitive to the reaction of the person you're calling. If he or she seems about to terminate the call, cut short your pitch and make arrangements to follow up with written material, a personal visit, or another telephone call.

- If you make a sale or get a personal appointment, end the conversation as quickly as possible. Talking too much is a dangerous habit.

- If you are rejected, politely thank the person for his or her time and get off the phone. Your consideration and courtesy may win you a longer hearing the next time you call.

- Make notes after every call. You learn something every time you dial, even if it's only what an executive doesn't want or need. You have little chance to establish a relationship on a future call if the person says, "I told you I wasn't interested the last time." You also have little chance to turn a prospect into a customer if you don't follow through on any promises you made during the conversation.

- Pick up the telephone again immediately. Cold calling is like learning to ride a horse—the longer you wait to get back in the saddle, the more that first fall hurts. Lots of practice is the key to becoming a pro.

Having no shame in contacting other people for legitimate business reasons will put you well on the road to success. But there's one other roadblock involving embarassment that may halt or limit you. This isn't a problem with other people's perceptions—rather, it's a problem with your perception of yourself.

Since I've become a broadcaster as well as a businessman, I've run into a lot of old friends. The most common question I'm asked first is not "How did you manage to get your own radio show?" or "How do you like broadcasting?" Rather, most people's initial reaction is to query, "Weren't you afraid you'd embarrass yourself?" That obviously reflects their own fears about making a fool of themselves by trying something outside their established areas of expertise.

I know, because that thought entered my own mind. I wouldn't be human if I hadn't imagined at least one scenario of my first show ending up on a blooper tape. On the other hand, I also had a vision of myself hosting the "Today Show." Neither was real, nor was either likely to come true.

What I was doing was following the same advice as we all give to our kids. And sound advice it is:

- You can do anything you put your mind to.
- Don't ever be afraid to try something new.
- If at first you don't succeed, try again.

Try as I can, I can't see any reason why I'm less likely to succeed in a new field or why I should be more afraid to try new things than I was when I was a kid. I'm more mature, more responsible, and have vastly more experience with the world than I did at age eighteen or age twenty-two. Instead of being ashamed of failing when I try something new, even if it's a radical departure from what I've been doing, I should be ashamed if I don't.

I did try broadcasting. Although I'll be the first to admit that my first show was far from perfect, I've become good enough to be awarded a five-fold increase in my air time and the chance to participate in broadcasting such events as the National Hockey League All-Star Game and Stanley Cup Finals, Major League Baseball Hall of Fame inductions, the AA and AAA All Star baseball games, the NFL Hall of Fame inductions, and others. I've also tried writing—I'll leave the judgment to you on how well I've done—and I'm expanding the time I devote to motivational speaking.

Maybe I have no shame—but I do have a lot of fun. You will, too, if you put embarassing yourself out of your mind.

Some Things to Think About

- Pursuing every avenue you can to promote yourself and your business is heroic. Evaluate your performance on how hard you tried, not on immediate results. If you expanded your horizons by taking actions you used to be hesitant to try, treat yourself as a hero. Soon you'll be acting like one all the time.

- Like putting a golf ball or shooting free throws, making cold calls is a skill that deteriorates rapidly without daily practice. Don't let yourself leave for the day until you've made enough calls to feel comfortable.

- Outside the office, get in the habit of trying things you used to fear would embarrass you. You'll have a lot of fun, and I guarantee you'll survive. The more you try, the easier it becomes.

Break the Rules
The Only S.O.P. You Should Accept Is That Which Increases Your B.O.T.T.O.M. L.I.N.E.

To be a success in business, be daring, be first, be different.
—Marchant

If you've paid any attention at all to recent Super Bowls (you've probably been locked up in a dungeon somewhere if you've avoided the hype), you're familiar with the no-huddle offense that has been so instrumental in getting the Buffalo Bills to the big game. This offense places a lot of pressure on the opposing defense, which has trouble getting situational players on and off the field in the much shorter time between plays. But I've noticed an irritation that goes beyond the tactical problems in the comments of many coaches. This irritation stems from their belief that Buffalo, Cincinnati, and other teams that occasionally run the no-huddle have broken the "rules"—not the official regulations of the game, but some sort of unwritten rule that by mutual agreement confined running plays without a huddle to the last two minutes of a half or of the game. In other words, Buffalo hasn't been playing fair.

I say, hurrah for Buffalo! I have nothing but respect for people who break rules that exist only because they make things easier for less creative, less tolerant, or less energetic people. Our society has benefited enormously from the courage of those who insisted that black Americans shouldn't have to sit in the back of the bus, that women shouldn't be restricted to nonexecutive positions, or that disabled people should not be denied access to buildings open to the rest of us. While you might not be up to civil disobedience or challenging the social establishment, you accomplish many more of your goals in life if you acquire some of the revolutionary spirit.

Let me give you a short example. When I became a distributor of fad merchandise, I found out that absolutely everyone in the business sold to retailers at a certain percentage above cost. This "rule" wasn't written down anywhere, but everyone accepted it because it made pricing easier and eliminated a lot of hard negotiation. There were no national fad distributors, but everyone told me that should I become one, I would still have to maintain this pricing structure.

Well, I did some financial projections based on that markup. Then I understood why there were no national distributors. I couldn't find a way I could provide a high level of service with the existing profit margins. So I had a choice: I could give up my goal of going national or I could change the rules.

I decided to increase the profit margin. In doing so, I added enormously to my work load. Instead of making easy deals, I had to negotiate fiercely when I bought and when I sold. My timing had to be perfect so I could sell when the market was hottest and I had the least price resistance. I had to make tough decisions about which products to carry—on some items no amount of negotiating would give me the rate of return I wanted. I was called every name in the book from crazy to unprintable. But I stuck to my guns. I not only became the only national distributor of fad merchandise, but a profitable one as well.

If you want to profit from trends, you have to acquire the same attitude. A new trend commonly involves unconventional behavior, unconventional ideas, or unconventional products. As strange as it sounds, many heads of movie studios scoffed at the idea that the public wanted to hear movie actors talk. Later, media experts couldn't see any reason the public would give up listening to their beloved radios to watch the tiny black and white pictures on those new-fangled television sets. However, the pioneers stuck to their guns and revolutionized the way we spend our leisure time.

In a small way, I revolutionized the way the fad business was conducted. I had my new ways of doing things, and they worked very well—almost too well. I was in danger of being as wedded to my new rules as my competitors had been to their old rules. But if

I hadn't broken my rules, I would have missed out on one of my most profitable fad lines.

The story begins in 1977 when a number of companies put on a big sales push for infant and toddler T-shirts with funny sayings silk-screened on the front. These companies reasoned that baby-boomer parents, who were hip and well-educated, would find these shirts irresistable. They were wrong. The merchandise bombed. I had personally thought the shirts were a great idea, and I had no idea why they failed to sell. I just remember being happy that I didn't heavily commit to a product until I was sure it would sell rather than trying to play soothsayer.

About a year later, I was in my booth at a national trade show in New York when I was approached by a most unconventional acquaintance. Steve Kaplan, with his shoulder-length hair and tattered clothing, looked like he had wandered in from Columbus Circle looking for a handout. He had the heaviest New York accent imaginable, and he talked so fast that his words were nearly incomprehensible. Most people shied away from Steve, but I knew that he was one of the all-time great "street hawkers." Even though he was still in his twenties, he had made himself financially secure for life peddling on the streets of New York.

Steve did tend to get carried away, though. When I finally got him to slow down, I found out that he was trying to get me to take a look at a line based on sayings for baby T-shirts. Instead of being silk-screened on the shirts, they were heat transfers that could be ironed on. Steve had at least twenty sayings such as TEETHING IS THE PITS, CAUTION: MAY BE WET AT BOTH ENDS, 90% ANGEL, 10% DEVIL, and HERE COMES TROUBLE. I thought the sayings were cute. But I had learned through observation and experience that once a fad idea bombs, it cannot be resuscitated. Many, many people had pitched me on variations of failed or exhausted fads, and I routinely turned them down. So I sent Steve on his way.

But Steve wouldn't give up. He came back and back and back to my booth, pleading with me to take a look. I saw so much of Steve I half expected him to be waiting in the men's room when I went there. But after I turned him away so many times, I began to think that maybe I was the one being stubborn. After all, how would it hurt me to set up a floor display of shirts in my booth. I finally said yes to Steve.

He introduced me to Sonny Crane of Golden Eagle Enterprises, the source of the heat transfers and the shirts. I had to admit the shirts looked good—the heat transfer produced a much more appealing look than silk-screening.

To my total and utter astonishment, we began writing orders for thousands of shirts at two dollars apiece. The year before, when the silk-screened shirts weren't moving, word traveled through the show like lightning and you could have detonated a bomb in the booths without hurting a buyer. This year the good news traveled equally as fast. Suddenly, I had achieved a new status as the genius who had uncovered the fad of the year.

By the end of the show, I knew that Sonny Crane's Golden Eagle Enterprises was at the beginning of what could be a meteoric rise. But I had serious doubts that he could arrange the cash flow necessary to produce the volume of shirts I could sell. If there wasn't sufficient product in the pipeline, the fad could die in infancy.

Another rule I had always followed was to negotiate the most favorable payment terms. But I decided that as long as I was breaking one rule, why not another? I insisted on giving Golden Eagle Enterprises C.O.D. certified checks, which would give them instant cash the day of each delivery. Sonny was delighted, and we shook hands on the deal. This also allowed me to purchase almost his entire inventory as his production came ready.

Shortly afterward, trucks began pulling up to my warehouse to discharge load after load of tiny T-shirts. The pace was frenzied, with many stores selling as many as twenty-four dozen shirts a week—that's twelve hundred dollars worth of merchandise. I share Mae West's belief that "Too much of a good thing is wonderful." It's my belief that you can never have too much of a good thing. In this case, the "good thing" was my monopoly on baby T-shirts.

But all good things must come to an end. The first problem was a shortage of American fabric, which slowed down Golden Eagle's production. That opened the door for less expensive Chinese and Pakistani shirts. I never considered switching suppliers, because I refused to risk my reputation for quality. But with American shirts in short supply, the poorer quality silk-screened shirts did reach the market through other distributors.

After a few months, I was surprised to find that baby T-shirts had made the transition from being a fad to being a trend. The market didn't disappear, even after the flood of imported merchandise. I now had forty different slogans, many in multicolored heat transfers. The difference between shirts with these transfers and the silk-screened version remained substantial, so I still shipped significant quantities of merchandise.

However, I was always on the alert to defend my market share. I had one account that had been ordering such huge quantities of shirts that I charged them $1.75 per shirt, twenty-five cents below my normal price. I found out that a manufacturer's representative who heard about my deal approached the buyer and promised him poor quality silk-screened shirts at $1.25 apiece. Worried that I would lose the account, I decided to break yet another rule—never savage your profit margin. I called the account and offered to drop the price of my shirts to match the other offer. The account gleefully accepted.

This time I had acted too hastily. I soon learned that my competitor would not have been able to ship the shirts when promised. However, I felt obligated to honor my low price. My profit was minimal, but I saved the account.

About the same time, I received a call from another buyer who threatened to return a large order because the T-shirts arrived scented in different fragrances. It didn't take me long to figure out that those shirts must have been stored next to the incense in our warehouse. I called the buyer back and jokingly said, "I won't charge you any extra for the scented shirts." To my surprise, the buyer's anger dissolved into pleasure. Thrilled at the bargain, she decided to keep the shirts—and ordered more.

I like to remind myself of the baby T-shirt story, especially now, when I'm often asked by the media to comment on potential fads. I don't find much use in peering into a crystal ball; on the other hand, if I answered every question from *Newsweek* or CNN by saying, "Well, we'll just have to wait and see," they'd never call me again. So I make an educated guess, using some rules of thumb I've observed. For example, I've found that merchandise spin-offs from a sequel never approach the sales from the original movie, no matter how well the sequel does at the box office. Reporters may find my predictions interesting, because they keep calling. I find it a lot of fun, like predicting the week's winners in the National Football League on my show.

But fun is fun and business is business. Baby T-shirts proved to me that when it comes to putting money where my mouth is, rules can go out the window. A fad, a trend, or a new idea can come from any unexpected place. For example, who would ever see millions of dollars in a grocery-store line? A man named Stew Leonard did. Here's his story.

Stew Leonard owned a small dairy in Norwalk, Connecticut. He delivered milk, but he noticed that customers liked to come to his place to pick up their dairy products. When he asked why, they told him their kids liked watching the machines fill bottles. Besides, Stew and his staff were very friendly, which made shopping a pleasure.

Stew Leonard could have been happy with this success. But he went on to ask his customers why they didn't like shopping in other places. Among their answers: narrow aisles, high prices for staples, unfriendly staff, and, most of all, standing in long lines at the checkout counter. When Stew did some investigating, he was told by industry experts that supermarkets had to be run the way they were because profit margins in the industry were so slim. Stew was told he would be crazy to try to change things.

But Stew decided to break all the rules. He started with two new rules, which he placed on a huge sign at the front door of his business:

RULE #1: THE CUSTOMER IS ALWAYS RIGHT.
RULE #2: IF THE CUSTOMER IS WRONG, REREAD RULE #1.

Then he went about breaking all the other rules. He built a cavernous store with aisles four times as wide as a normal supermarket. He bought oversized shopping carts and hired one employee just to make sure they were clean.

To cut prices on staples, he cut down on selection—instead of carrying five brands of ketchup, he carried one. But he bought in such huge quantities that he could charge much less than other grocers. He bought his own fruits and vegetables directly from suppliers, which meant the produce in his store was fresher than that in most supermarket chains. He had his own bakery, his own butcher shop, and, of course, his own dairy.

Next, he worked on making shopping fun. He built and stocked a petting zoo for the kids. He filled the store with animated animals that sang songs and talked to the customers. He put out lots of free samples. And he built a glass-walled milk bottling room so customers could watch.

Finally, he addressed the problem of checkout lines. Instead of ten or twelve lanes, Stew's store had forty, and he kept them manned. No matter how crowded his store got, customers were on their way within minutes of stepping up to a cash register.

Other grocers waited for Stew Leonard to go bankrupt. Instead, he drew customers from twenty, thirty miles away. His business expanded to two superstores that annually produce several times the revenue—and profit—of the average supermarket.

You may not have the skill or resources to open a large food store, but you can still find a niche if you look hard. I recently found another example in a small town. Several small video stores had done adequate business in town for years. Then a major video chain opened a huge superstore in a local shopping center. Business at some of the small stores plummeted as much as 70 percent. The very friendly, aggressive owner of one of those stores saw his revenue nearly cut in half. Many people told him the situation was hopeless, because he couldn't cut his prices to match the chain store's or order thirty copies of every new release to match their stock. The only way he felt he could compete was to offer the one service the chain couldn't—home delivery of videotapes. But, again, the naysayers said that delivery would be so expensive customers would have to pay double for tapes.

But the owner found a way. He went out and signed up local restaurants, dry cleaners, a convenience store, and a pharmacy to form a home-delivery network. Customers could order a movie, a pizza, a prescription, and a half gallon of milk in one call. Then he found a computerized phone system that would handle the orders without requiring a staff person. The computer answered the phone, took the order, then faxed it to the vendors involved. As a result, the owner cut the price of a delivery to just $1.50. Response was overwhelming, and his video store continued to prosper.

Playing by the accepted rules gives all the advantages to established companies that have a vested interest in retaining their market share. If you want to break through to success, you'll have to find a way to break the rules.

Some Things to Think About

- Practice thinking about breaking the rules when you're purchasing a product or service. What's annoying about the way your auto repair shop schedules appointments? What's inconvenient about taking time to get your hair cut? What information isn't readily available when you're shopping for a new appliance? Asking questions may lead to profitable ideas.

- Pay attention to your frustration level at work. If you regularly find a particular task or procedure tedious or unproductive, it may be because it involves an unnecessary rule.

- Focus on deciphering the difference between constructive and destructive comments from your employer, co-workers or others in your line of work. Criticism that includes the phrase "because that's the way we've always done things" should be examined with particular care.

Taylor's Pyramid Planning
The First Thing You Should Do Every Day Is the Thing That Will Get the Most Weight Off Your Shoulders

A successful person has the habit of doing the things failures don't like to do.

—E. M. Gray

Some mornings when I open the door to my office I feel like a cowboy who awakens to find a stampede heading straight toward him. Thanks to the wonders of modern communication, there's often a wild herd of faxes, telephone messages, letters, shipping manifests, and other pieces of paper that seem to be racing toward me. My first instinct, like that of the drowsy cowboy, is to expend my energy dodging one "cow" after another. But the cowboy and I know both that we'd better stop dodging and get the herd under control so we can move in an orderly fashion toward our goals.

Earlier in this book, when talking about the use of time, I explained that I valued effectiveness over efficiency. Being the most effective person I can be means I'm willing to drop absolutely everything at a moment's notice to pursue an opportunity that may arise today, because that opportunity may not be available tomorrow. Any businessperson who hesitates subordinating a schedule to seize a chance to find a new product, gain an advantage on competitors, or make personal strides is an ineffective businessperson.

However, my willingness to throw my schedule aside as neces-

sary doesn't mean that I don't strongly believe in planning my
days. In fact, I have a passion for efficiency and order. Capitaliz-
ing on a fad or a trend requires acting quickly and decisively,
which is impossible if your energies are partially wasted or misdirected. As I've already explained several times, my company is
capable of handling a ten-fold increase in business overnight
while still meeting our goal of shipping out every order the day
it's received. I've been able to create and maintain this unusual
level of service with the assistance of a time-management system
I've developed over the years. This system helps me accomplish
what I have to do, especially in coping with the volume of telephone calls, correspondence, sales calls, and other demands that
fill my day.

My time-management system begins with reserving time for
planning every single day. I make sure I take this time when I'm
at my physical and mental peak, not when I'm tired or distracted
by problems or other people. For me, the best time is the morning, before I arrive at the office. I get up early every single day,
then go for a run. The exercise, followed by a hot shower, makes
me wide awake and energetic. Then, before my family gets up, I
sit down to organize my day.

When I plan, I use some techniques and tools common to other
good time-management systems. One of these techniques is the
to-do list. In my case, this is a comprehensive master list of
reminders of everything I have to do or have promised I'd do.
You'll remember that I have constantly stressed the importance of
doing what I say I'll do, whether it involves shipping an order,
paying an invoice, dealing with an employee, or providing information. Every single one of these commitments, plus my other
obligations, winds up on my master list.

I don't bother arranging the entries in any order of priority
when I make this list. Instead, it's purely chronological, with a
date at the top of each page. This system could become cumber-
some if it weren't for a very good habit I've developed over the
years: I try my best to deal and dispose of every communication
when it reaches me. This technique involves:

• Touching every piece of paper just once. Except for
  clippings, catalogs, or other reference material, I hardly

ever file anything away for future action. If a letter or fax requests information, I provide it immediately. Many times I find making a telephone call is more effective and less time consuming than dictating a reply. If the correspondence requires a decision, I try to make one on the spot. I've become so adept that I never again see 95 percent of the paper that arrives on my desk.

- Taking telephone calls whenever possible. If my staff takes a message, half the time I end up playing telephone tag. I save an enormous amount of time not having to return calls.

- Following through on promises I've made immediately. If I've promised some information, a price list, or a delivery during a telephone call, I make good immediately upon hanging up. If I make a commitment during a personal sales call, I normally call my office as soon as possible to give instructions for following through. When I get back to the office, I'm free to tackle anything that's accumulated during my absence.

I should point out that I write everything I've promised to do on my master list, even if I accomplish the task right away. This creates a permanent dated record that is easy to consult later.

During my morning planning time, I review my to-do list. I pay special attention to incomplete tasks that have been pending for a while, normally because I'm waiting for information or for someone else to act. I make a note on today's list to follow up, cross-referencing the date of the original entry.

I've become quite efficient in making sure my to-do list is complete. I'm human, so I occasionally forget to do things, but I almost never forget to write them down.

The second tool I use in my daily planning is my appointment book. I'm a fanatic about being on time. One of my close friends says he asks me to call him at 10:00 A.M. every once in a while so he can reset his clocks. He's teasing me, but I don't care—I cultivate a reputation for being reliable. Every morning, I make sure that any appointments, meetings, or other time-related activities on my to-do list are entered in the appropriate places in my appointment book. When I get to the office, I make a photocopy of that day's page so that my secretary knows where I'll be or what I'm doing at all times.

As you know, I'm not hesitant to disrupt my schedule when necessary. Since my secretary has all the information, it's easy for me to have her cancel or reschedule any commitments. However, I do try to follow through with telephone calls or other non-time-consuming activities even if my priorities for the day have drastically changed. I'll take ten minutes off to follow up with a customer or do a radio interview. I don't like putting off for another day anything I can do today.

Doing today what should be done today brings up the final, and by far the most important, element in my time-management system—placing in order activities that will fill the majority of the day when I'm not scheduled for an appointment. I've read a lot of systems for determining priorities. Most revolve around writing down one's lifetime goals and short-term goals, organizing one's list of daily activities in accordance with these goals, then assigning priorities such as *A activities*, *B activities*, etc.

The key concept in my method, which I believe is a lot simpler, involves the word *pyramid*. No, don't groan. I'm not talking about the structure, which is produced by laying a solid foundation, then building toward a pinnacle. You've no doubt been introduced to the financial-planning pyramid and the career-planning pyramid and the marketing pyramid. I'm as bored with these as you are.

But to me, the pyramids are a symbol of mankind's capacity for superhuman achievement. I believe that landing men on the moon was a stunning triumph. But I understand that it was accomplished through skillful melding of modern technological advances. It's something I can imagine myself participating in if I were a scientist.

The building of the pyramids without the use of machinery is another story altogether. Shaping, moving, and lifting those massive stones required harnessing the energies of thousands of people to accomplish the most excruciating of physical labors over a period of time spanning twenty to forty years. Although we may find the goal of devoting all that labor to building a monument to one person sadly misdirected, we can still stand in awe of the achievement of men who faced the most unpleasant tasks day after day after day.

You and I don't have any five-ton blocks of stone to move every day. But we all have tasks that weigh us down by causing worry or anxiety. Worry and anxiety are the most damaging of emotions. They sap both time and energy. They also produce a negative mind-set that makes every task seem more onerous during the course of the day.

Unfortunately, worry and anxiety seem to be addictive. Putting off tasks that weigh heavily on the mind seems to be far more common than dealing with those tasks promptly. Avoidance may cause temporary relief, but the situation inevitably worsens down the line. Eventually, worry and anxiety become paralyzing.

Like everyone else, I worry. And I usually worry about the most important tasks I face. So when I sit down to plan my day, I go over unfinished tasks one by one. Any that awaken that familiar feeling in the pit of my stomach, I tackle first.

Doing first what takes the most weight off my shoulders has several benefits. First, I solve a lot of little problems before they become big problems. For example, I may find out on Monday that a shipment will probably be delayed, which means I can't deliver to my customers on Friday, as promised. I could do nothing, hoping I'll get lucky and be able to fulfill my commitment. But if I'm unlucky, I will have very angry accounts to pacify. So I pick up the phone on Monday and alert all my customers. Invariably, they appreciate the advance notice. And if, in fact, I can ship on time, I'm a hero, too.

Secondly, successfully coping with my biggest problems first gives me a rush of adrenaline that propels me through the rest of the day. I'm more relaxed and confident, a state of mind that I've found makes me much more receptive to new products and new ideas. Worried, anxious people listen primarily to what's going on inside their own heads, not to what other people are saying.

I've followed this simple time-management system for many years and it's become second nature. I've gotten so used to dealing with problems directly that I don't think of them as unpleasant any more, just as I'm sure the thousands of people who labored on the pyramids adapted to the grueling work. But following my system is easy only if I do it every single day. As with exercise, a few days off makes getting back in the routine much more painful.

Adopting a system like mine is bound to make you more

efficient, even if your line of work is substantially different from mine. Recently, I was explaining my system during a seminar when a man stood up and said, "Stu, have you ever considered the fact that your system may work only because your business lends itself to quick action? My work involves researching and writing complex reports that may take months, even years to complete. I can't process each piece of paper just once."

A few years ago the man's question might have stumped me. But I was already at work on this book, which might be considered one great big giant report. When I first signed the contract to write the book, the work ahead seemed overwhelming. But after a little thought, I decided that it would be like any other job if I just chopped it up into small enough parts. I decided the way to proceed was to devote time to it every single day. At first, I found it hard to talk about my life, my work, and my principles. So I scheduled one hour early in the morning, to get it out of the way. Later, when I was more comfortable, I put in my time whenever it was convenient.

This methodical approach payed off. I made much faster progress than I ever thought I would. And a task that was very difficult when I began eventually became one of the highlights of my day. If you concentrate on getting the weight off your shoulders as soon as possible, you'll accomplish more than you could possibly imagine every day.

Some Things to Think About

- Buy a spiral-bound notebook for your to-do lists—you won't lose any pages, and it's easy to carry around. Concentrate on writing down every task, no matter how menial (e.g., pick up a box of printer ribbons, send a congratulations letter to a customer who's a proud new father, etc.). You'll miss a lot at first, but after a month your list will be comprehensive.

- If you have trouble overcoming your urge to put off dealing with unpleasant situations, try writing two "what if" scenarios. First, write down everything you can imagine, good and bad, that might happen if you act immediately. Then write down what might happen, good or bad, if you procrastinate. If you're honest, you'll invariably find that acting now is a lot less frightening than acting later.

- If you've got a lot of problems you're worried about, tackle them one by one. The good feeling that comes from resolving one situation will propel you into the second with newfound confidence.

Taylor's Law
Everything That Can Go Wrong Will Go Wrong—If You Expect It To

> There is no medicine like hope, no incentive so great, and
> no tonic as powerful as the expectation of something
> tomorrow.
>
> —O. S. Marden

Murphy's Law may have been offered in jest, but I hear it quoted almost exclusively by people who incorporate this bit of "wisdom" in their philosophy of life as well as in their business planning. I find nothing wrong in trying to evaluate sources of potential problems in launching a new venture, a new product line, a new marketing program, or similar activity. But taking Murphy's law seriously means approaching business with a fundamentally negative attitude. The implication is that it would be a miracle if things didn't go wrong. As I said earlier, I've never met a successful person who thought success depended on luck.

Taylor's Law, on the other hand, is grounded on the belief that you're far more likely to be successful if you think you will. And unlike Murphy, I can back mine up with scientific research. As I've mentioned before, I was an experimental psychology major in college. I still have a lot of respect and fondness for the discipline, and I keep my eyes open for the latest news in the field. That's why I know that in the last few years, psychological research has pointed to optimism as the key to success in life.

One example is a study done by Dr. Charles R. Snyder of the University of Kansas that was reported in the *Journal of Personality and Social Psychology*. Dr. Snyder and his colleagues followed 3,920 college students from their registration as freshmen through completion of their college years. To the researchers' surprise, they discovered that by far the best predictor of success in college was not S.A.T. scores or high school grades—the two measurements relied on most heavily for college admissions. Rather, the best predictor was hope, a freshman's level of optimism that he or she would succeed. Dr. Snyder commented, "Students with high hopes set themselves higher goals and know how to work to attain them. When you compare students of equivalent intellectual aptitude and past academic achievements, what sets them apart is hope." Also, your level of expectation should always be higher than your achievement level.

Several other studies shatter the myth that the people who cope best with serious adversity are those who expect it. Two separate studies, one of people who suffered paralysis from spinal cord injuries and one of people with serious diseases like congestive heart failure, found that optimists lived longer, suffered less depression, and achieved for greater than normal levels of rehabilitation than people with negative outlooks. Another study of eighty-one rehabilitation nurses showed that their level of optimism had a substantial effect on the recovery of the patients with whom they worked.

Scientific research has confirmed what I've believed for years. I'm not a Pollyanna, but if attitudes were religions, I'd be a confirmed optimist. I plan for success and believe wholeheartedly that I will be successful. Hope energizes me, and it also tends to energize those with whom I come into contact. I haven't conducted any controlled psychological studies, but I have participated in or witnessed several classic cases in which the expection of success played a critical role in achieving success.

The one that comes to mind most readily is one of the most remarkable marketing phenomena of the last decade—the New Kids on the Block. These young men not only soared to the top of the music charts and set box-office records on tour, they were also featured in the best-selling music merchandise spin-offs of all time.

If you walk around any mall and pay attention to what teenagers are wearing, it seems like half have apparel connected to a rock star or rock group. But almost all of the rock T-shirts and posters are either sold outside concert halls or in stores that specialize in that merchandise. Over the last two decades, I've had very little success trying to sell such merchandise in the fad market—with two exceptions.

The first was Michael Jackson. As a member of the Jackson Five, he'd been a familiar figure in the music business for years. I don't think anyone had a clue that *Thriller* would generate such explosive sales. When Jackson's album catapulted to the top of the charts, a ferocious demand for merchandise arose immediately. I plunged into the frenzy to compete for merchandise, and I sold everything I could get my hands on. This fad was very profitable, but like most others, only lasted a few months. Six months later, I would have had trouble giving away a Michael Jackson poster.

New Kids on the Block was different. Their success may have caught the public by surprise. But in reality it had been carefully orchestrated from the very beginning by a man named Maurice Starr.

Starr's inspiration was the success of the Latin teenage group Menudo. Menudo's members were all young teenage boys— retirement from the group was mandatory on one's sixteenth birthday. The group's tours generated millions of dollars in their home, Puerto Rico, and throughout Latin America. Menudo's occasional appearances in New York produced near riots as pre-teenage girls stormed their hotels and lined up outside concert halls.

Looking back, it's hard to believe that the success of Menudo continued for years without an American counterpart. But pre-teenage girls—girls who are post-Barbie, but pre-puberty—were one of the most ignored markets in the country. Boys that age generated large sales of baseball cards, sports equipment such as skateboards, and other sports-related merchandise. But even though babysitting tended to give ten-, eleven-, and 12-year-old girls money to spend, they had little to spend it on.

Maurice Starr decided to aim for that audience. He carefully recruited five white, clean-cut Boston area teenagers with little previous show business experience. He chose them not primarily for their ability to sing, but for their dancing ability, personality, and looks. The music, based on the black soul sound, was simple and "clean." But the performances of the five members of the group were elaborately choreographed to energize young audiences.

From the very beginning, Starr's expectations were achieving the blockbuster success in the U.S. that Menudo had achieved in Latin America. Unlike most promoters, he didn't concentrate solely on producing one hit record to launch the group. Rather, he planned a coordinated approach that combined recording, touring, books, and merchandise sales.

I'm sure the marketing campaign for New Kids on the Block will be studied in business schools for years to come. Unlike most other fads, the sales of New Kids merchandise built rather slowly. Since I'm headquartered in the Boston area, I was aware of them before many others in my industry. I began to carry the merchandise, which was in plentiful supply.

That situation began to change as the popularity of New Kids rose. Preteenage girls poured into stores desperate for anything connected with their idols. And to my surprise, the demand didn't end in a few months. The New Kids racked up gross revenues of more than $50 million dollars for each of two years, and merchandise sales stayed strong throughout the entire period.

The phenomenon attracted so much attention that I was invited to appear on a TV show with the mothers of the New Kids to discuss it. Others on the show focused on Starr's shrewd appraisal of the potential market and his skillful training of the group. When it was my turn, I focused on Starr's high expectations of success. If he hadn't been completely optimistic, he could not have devoted the intense energy to the project, energy that translated into stunning public performances. More than anything, his exceptional level of hope produced the exceptional level of success.

In my business, I have much more frequently seen good ideas and potentially profitable tie-ins fail because of hesitancy or lukewarm enthusiasm. Many more products fail than succeed, which can be discouraging. When that discouragement permeates the attitude of salespeople, it virtually guarantees future failure. Nothing turns me off more than a salesperson who tells me, "This product is clever and well-made. Who knows, maybe it will sell a little."

I think it's particularly unfortunate that some very brilliant people who have achieved only limited success take perverse pride in modest achievement, flaunting a "who cares if I'm successful" attitude like a badge. I think a prime example of this attitude is the story of the TV show "Twin Peaks." This show was created by David Lynch, a gifted director who had achieved a certain cult status with movies such as *Eraserhead* and *Blue Velvet.* The premier of "Twin Peaks" was so stunning and so different that it instantly became a phenomenon. The show made the covers of *Time* and *Newsweek,* and if you couldn't participate in speculation about who killed Laura Palmer, you were distinctly out of touch.

I thought "Twin Peaks" had substantial merchandising potential if it became a long-running series. But all the public clamor seemed to produce either a fear or resentment of success in Lynch and his staff. Instead of courting their audience, they began to mock, even irritate it. The "who killed Laura Palmer" plot went on so long it eventually bored most of the audience, and the eventual answer was so weird it turned off many of the remaining fans. The last show, which was seemingly designed to show viewers that they were idiots for having gotten involved in the first place, was one of the five lowest rated shows of the week.

You may think I'm a little harsh on David Lynch. After all, no one should be forced to achieve commercial fame and success. But I'm writing this book for people who want to succeed, not for people who are satisfied with failing or with "good trys." I want to demonstrate the power of optimism and the destructive effects of negative thinking.

This book is an example of how optimism can produce enthusiasm that leads to success. When I decided to write a book, I had absolutely no connections in publishing. I knew that if I completed a manuscript and sent it around to publishing companies on my own, the odds of it being accepted were more than one thousand to one. I also knew that if I waited for someone to come to me and ask me to write the book, my odds would be a lot longer than that.

After some thought, I decided on a two-pronged approach. I took some time each day and began writing. Since I'm not a writer, I found the process excruciating. But I knew that no one would take me seriously unless I actually began putting words on paper. Because I expected to succeed, I was able to stick with it day after day. Eventually, I turned out more than one hundred pages of text.

Secondly, I began to talk about my book to everyone I met. I never understood would-be authors who try to keep their project secret, as if the act of writing were embarrassing. I worked my network of contacts. Eventually, this linkage worked. I was able to arrange a meeting with Tony Seidl and Dave Weiner. Tony started out his career as a book salesman and had risen to become a publisher. He was currently working as a book agent and packager. Dave, Tony's partner, was the author/packager of more than one hundred books.

I subsequently learned that professionals like Tony and Dave hear from dozens of people a week who want to write a book. But my enthusiasm, plus the fact that I'd already put pen to paper, impressed them enough to schedule a meeting. My expectations of success were catching, and they arranged for me to obtain the professional services of a writer with more than seventy books to his credit. Even though most unpublished authors have to finish an entire manuscript to get the attention of a publishing company, our four-man team put together a fifty page proposal and obtained a contract from a major New York publishing house.

I was pleased, but not surprised. I always expect to succeed, plan to succeed, and work with full enthusiasm toward that success. If you want to get ahead in any field, that attitude is a must.

Some Things to Think About

- Record your sales calls, telephone conversations, and meetings. When you play back the tapes, listen for negative comments. You'll be surprised how many times you find yourself saying things like, "This may not work, but what if we try . . ." Nervousness leads us to many unconscious negative statements. You'll eliminate them only if you become fully aware of what you're saying.

- Give yourself pep talks. During my early morning planning time, I often mentally list reasons why the day ahead will be successful. To practice, you might want to write down a list of reasons to be optimistic. Never, ever write down negative thoughts.

- Surround yourself with positive people. An acquaintance of mine, a very bright executive, is also one of the grumpiest, most unhappy people I've come in contact with. I was puzzled about the reason for his attitude—until I met his business associates. Even I would have had trouble keeping up my enthusiasm in the face of their complaining and sarcasm. I believe this man has little chance to rise further in this field until he separates himself from the attitude of the people around him.

The Ugly Executive
Today's Most Fatal Business Disease Is the Inability to Pick Up the Phone and Say Hello

> First we form habits, then they form us. Conquer your bad habits or they'll eventually conquer you.
> —Dr. Rob Gilbert

Recently I was sitting in my office a little after five when my secretary said that I had a call from a man whose name I didn't recognize. My day had been absolutely brutal. The guest I had scheduled for my talk show that evening had abruptly cancelled, and it had taken me many calls to find a suitable replacement. I sandwiched those calls between a stream of major and minor problems. By the end of the day, all I could think about was fitting in a nap to regain the energy I'd need to do my show at ten o'clock that night. The last thing I wanted to do was to talk to anyone else, especially if it was a salesman. I felt like telling Cecile to tell the caller I'd left for the day. But at the last second I summoned up the will to overcome temptation. I hate being given the runaround on the phone, and I have always made it a firm rule to talk to anyone who called unless I was legitimately tied up. So I picked up the phone.

The caller whose name I hadn't recognized turned out to be a New York businessman whose wife is a well-known network television personality. One of his companies had developed a very interesting novelty item that he wanted to market. He explained that he decided to call me not only because I was a national distributor, but because people had told him I was always willing to listen to new ideas. We talked for nearly an hour, and when I finally hung up I had not only picked up a potentially lucrative product, but had also opened the door for future networking that might provide broadcasting or publishing opportunities.

What would have been wrong with letting my secretary take his name so I could call him back the next day? Maybe nothing. On the other hand, he could have called somebody else before I got back to him. I also wouldn't have been able to demonstrate just how accessible I am by taking the call promptly and listening patiently while he made his sales pitch. He would have formed a different first impression from the one I would have wanted him to form. First impressions are crucial in today's sluggish economy. If someone can't get through to you, you can be sure one of your competitors will be glad to pick up the phone and take the new product or new account away from you.

Now, I realize that I'd be hard pressed to find a businessperson who deliberately turns away new business because he or she doesn't answer the phone. Instead, most would argue that their telephone habits stem from the practical necessity to organize and filter input. It's true that none of us could accomplish anything if we tried to give our full attention to everyone who wanted it. We can't read every professional journal or every memo, we can't attend every convention or cocktail party, we can't sit in on every meeting or planning session. One key to all of the effective time-management systems I've read is the ability to say no.

However, the necessity of organizing and filtering input is far more obvious than the dangers involved in the process. On a practical level, most businesspeople have a tendency to talk only to people they know, about subjects they want to talk about. They respond to every buzz from their secretaries with, "Who is it?" and "What does he want?" In an effort to save themselves time and prevent "surprises," they try to decide if a conversation is going to be important before it takes place.

This may be efficient in the short run, but it's disastrous in the long run. The reason: It's nearly impossible to learn anything this way. The line between legitimately limiting people's access to you and becoming isolated from what's really happening in your business, or is about to happen, is razor-thin. To me, it's spending your life walking around on a twelve-inch window ledge outside the thirtieth floor of a building. The feeling of control is exhilarating—but a misstep is fatal.

I was recently reminded of the importance of being accessible and not being afraid of what people had to say by the death of retailing legend Sam Walton, founder of Wal-Mart. Before parceling out his wealth to his children shortly before his death, Walton was the richest man in America, with a net worth estimated at $8 billion. But despite these fabulous riches, Walton never spent a minute ensconced in a fancy office cordoned off by a phalanx of secretaries and administrative assistants. Instead, he spent many of his days prowling the floors of his stores, talking to any employee or customer who had something to say. When he was in his modest office, his strict open-door policy provided access to anyone. Any management efficiency expert would call this schedule eccentric or crazy. But the results? While dozens of retailing giants like Gimbels and Macy's were spiraling into bankruptcy, Wal-Mart annually posted huge sales gains. Despite its size, Walton structured his company to provide customers today with what they want today. He also structured his internal policies and procedures to allow his store managers and employees to provide the level of service necessary to attract and retain customers.

In the days after Mr. Walton's death, I read numerous tributes to him penned by dozens of chief executives of giant corporations. Without exception, they labeled him an "innovator," a "genius." Although Sam Walton deserved the praise, I couldn't help but react to the hypocrisy in these statements. I suspected not one of these multimillion-dollar-a-year magnates had ever spent a minute considering adding more customer contact to his schedule or implementing an open-door policy. As a result, most major U.S. companies continue to lose business to more aggressive foreign firms as well as to entrepreneurs here at home.

No better example exists of the results of isolation than Roger Smith, the former chairman of General Motors. Mr. Smith reportedly reached his lofty position at the head of the nation's largest industrial firm by becoming the most accomplished bureaucrat in a corporation legendary for its bureaucracy. Long after huge losses and a declining market share should have awakened management to the fact that the company had lost touch with its market, GM resisted change. Finally, Roger Smith became an object of ridicule through the critical success of the documentary movie *Roger and Me*, a biting chronicle of a Flint, Michigan, filmmaker's numerous attempts to interview Smith about the effects of closing down a GM plant in that town. Soon afterward, the company's board of directors initiated forced management changes to start the massive process of reorganizing a company that had become a symbol of ineffective management.

Obviously, it doesn't take a genius to figure out that I wouldn't have gotten to first base in the fad business if I had isolated myself. In fact, you could build a hilarious Bob Newhart comedy routine around my trying to prescreen my calls:

"You mean, the guy wants to talk to me about selling rocks as pets?"

"This lunatic has these slimy robots and dinosaurs that grow in water?"

"Come on, some woman wants to print pictures on shoelaces?"

You can't help but laugh when you think about how ridiculous Pet Rocks, Gro-Bots, and designer shoelaces must have seemed before they became hot fads. But then, if you think about it, what would you have thought if someone had suggested that:

- You could see almost any movie you'd like by slipping a tape into a machine on top of your TV.
- You could insert a document into a machine on your desk and have it appear an instant later in a machine on a desk three thousand miles away.
- You could fit the contents of a twenty-five-volume encyclopedia plus video and audio explanations on a disk smaller than a 45 record.

Today VCRs, fax machines, and compact disks are part of our lives, not crazy ideas or fads. But you'll never get in on the next fad or innovation if you're not willing to talk to people who may, at first, sound more than a bit crazy.

I've found that picking up the phone has paid off in other ways than just in finding new products. One story began about a year ago when I stopped by the booth of a casual business acquaintance at a trade show. My acquaintance introduced me to a customer who owned a chain of retail stores, a man I'll call Bill Jones. After a few minutes of polite conversation, Bill and I discovered that his stores might be the perfect outlet for some merchandise I was looking to sell. We had coffee that day, and had two or three fruitful conversations during the next two weeks. We appeared to be close to signing a deal when, suddenly, Bill stopped taking my calls. I left a dozen messages over the course of a month without getting a return call or any explanation. I was at a loss to figure out what had happened.

Then, one day, I got a call from the head of a collection agency. Solicitation calls from collection agencies offering to handle my delinquent accounts come in every day. But I always answer the phone if I'm not otherwise occupied, and this time I was glad I did. I learned that the casual acquaintance who had introduced me to Bill Jones had defaulted on a large debt. Jones had assumed, erroneously, that I was a close associate of the deadbeat and had cut me off. Guilt by association!

As soon as I got off the phone, I dictated a letter and had it faxed to Bill Jones along with a copy of my credit report. An hour later Bill called to apologize, and we concluded a very profitable deal on the spot—a deal that never would have taken place if I hadn't picked up the telephone.

You may want to be the chief executive of a Fortune 500 company—but you shouldn't try to get there by acting like one. Answering your phone is courteous, effective, and surprisingly, efficient. Having your secretary take a message does not necessarily save you time. You have to read the message and schedule time to return the call. More often than not, the person you're calling is now out of the office or occupied, so a frustrating and time-consuming game of telephone tag begins.

The most ridiculous affectation of all is having a secretary place a call for you. It saves absolutely no time, because you sit in your office waiting for the call to go through. If you're not the president of the United States, you're sending a message that you're pretentious.

Even dodging salespeople can be more time consuming than taking their calls. I'm a salesman too, and a persistent one. If a prospective customer won't take my call, I'll keep calling back until I get through. However, if the executive I'm trying to reach takes my call and tells me he's not interested, I'll respond by scratching him off my list and moving on. A single two- or three-minute call saves both of us time in the future.

If I had to sum up my philosophy about telephone calls, I'd say it's courtesy and curiosity. In more than two decades of experience, I've found that being accessible and courteous on the phone is infectious. I have far less trouble getting through to people once they've found out how easy it is to get me on the phone. It seems that under the guise of seeming efficient and important, we've developed a national case of telephone bad manners that's crippled effective communications. Simple courtesy is part of the remedy.

But the courtesy to pick up the phone doesn't mean that you'll get the most out of the call. I've found that maintaining a sense of curiosity is equally important. When I reach for the telephone, my attitude is, "I wonder what I'll learn from this call?" If you resent a call, or expect it to be tedious or boring, you've partially stopped listening before you say hello. The same is true if you try to be "efficient" by reviewing paperwork while you talk—again, you're prejudging the call before you begin to listen.

I'm an effective salesman because I feel a sense of excitement just before I call on a customer. I'm a good listener because I try to generate that same sense of excitement before I pick up the phone. Above all, I don't let the reality that the call may be routine affect my listening ability to the point where I don't respond correctly when a call *isn't* routine. If a call offers an opportunity, I've made an excellent first impression and approached the call with an attitude that insures I'll recognize opportunity when it's presented.

Some Things to Think About

- Keep a telephone log. This not only provides an excellent record of all your calls, but it also allows you to review those calls. At the end of the week, add up the number of calls that really turned out to be useless, and calculate the time spent on those calls. You'll be surprised how low those numbers are.

- Make sure your new telephone habits also become the telephone habits of your staff, even those who only answer during lunch hour or at other random hours. *Your* image suffers when someone representing you makes a bad impression on the telephone.

- When you call someone, be prepared to take notes on the way your call is handled. If you are impressed with anything about the way the call was handled, make notes and incorporate the techniques into your habits.

The Real Art of the Deal
The Key Is How Well You Buy, Not How Well You Sell

A penny saved is a penny earned.
—Benjamin Franklin

Whenever I think about the subject of buying and selling, I'm reminded of the story of two guys who decided to go into the pumpkin business. They drove their truck to the country, found a farm, and bought an entire truckload for one dollar apiece. They drove back to the city, parked by the roadside, and set up a sign that read PUMPKINS $1. Business was brisk, and in a couple of hours the truck was empty. Then one of the guys stopped to calculate their earnings.

His friend asked, "So how much did we make?"

The first guy replied, "We didn't make a cent."

Disgusted, the friend said, "See, I told you we should have bought two loads."

As silly as this story seems, I've encountered more than a few entrepreneurs who run their businesses about the same way. They get so caught up in the excitement of buying and selling that they forget that the fundamental principle of making a profit is insuring the maximum possible margin between the cost of goods purchased and the costs of goods sold. If that margin is not sufficiently large, even designers of the most clever products and the creators of the most dazzling marketing campaigns are doomed to failure.

My priority has always been buying. I learned this from an early age by tagging along with my father. As I've explained before, his business was buying and selling distressed goods—in

111

other words, products other companies were unable to sell at a profit. My father never handled anything that generated consumer demand like *Batman* T-shirts or *Saturday Night Fever* posters. The only way he could sell merchandise was if the price was sufficiently low. That meant buying at a price that was even lower.

In years of watching my father drive from factory to factory and from town to town, I learned the value of two personal characteristics—patience and discipline. Many times I felt myself becoming swayed by the attractiveness of a particular lot of merchandise, by the unusual persuasiveness or charm of the seller, or by the fact that we were tired of being on the road. None of these factors influenced my father. He would not buy until the price reached a certain point he had in mind. That price was one that allowed him to go back home and get a good night's sleep, because he knew he was guaranteed a profit. The selling of the merchandise didn't concern him—his genius for buying right was the key factor in the success of his business over decades.

The buying and selling decisions in my business are more complicated than were my father's decisions. My father had virtually no overhead and absolutely no sales staff—it didn't cost him money to wait days or weeks for the right deal. But through painful experience I have found that the same principle of buying at a price that will produce a profit still applies. Like those proverbial two guys in the pumpkin business, I've found that taking a deal simply to meet my overhead somehow ends up costing me money. The harder I concentrate on buying—and the more patience and discipline I show—the higher my profits. Those profits, in turn, allow me to have even more patience and exercise more discipline the next time around.

Over the years, I've developed a very structured approach to buying for my business. This approach features four different buying strategies based on four specific circumstances.

Buying Situation One: *Purchasing a Product That's in Great Demand*

The easiest product to sell is one that everyone is clamoring to buy. That's why I'm in the fad business. When a fad is raging, I don't have to spend money advertising or marketing—my phones are ringing with more orders than I can possibly fill.

Of course, so are the phones of the suppliers of the merchandise I need. When I buy in this situation, price is not the main consideration. The demand insures that I will obtain the profit margin I need. It also means that I can't use price as leverage in obtaining merchandise.

What I can use as leverage is my ability to pay and pay quickly. When I told the story of the *Batman* fad, I explained how my ability to pay for merchandise C.O.D. leap-frogged me in front of others who would pay in thirty or sixty days. Cash and a top-flight credit rating can do wonders.

But this is not the only strategy you can use. Perhaps the most important assets you have are your character and dedication to the product. When everyone is offering money, you need to make yourself attractive by emphasizing the intangibles. You want the buyer to know you are in business for the long run, not just to make a quick buck. You want to emphasize that you want to establish a long-term relationship, a relationship you have every intention of continuing after the current fad has passed. You want to pledge that selling the product under discussion is the primary focus of your business efforts, that you believe in the product, and that the maximum profit for both of you will be the result.

It's hard to sell character if you haven't demonstrated character in your previous business relationships. References from other companies that have profited from trusting you are invaluable when suppliers have to make important decisions. The balance in your bank account may go up and down with your business fortunes, but your reputation should be something that is always being enhanced and cultivated.

That means following through on your promises, including the promise to maintain a long-term relationship. If a supplier comes through for you when you desperately need product, you have to come through for the supplier when they need a sale six months or a year down the road. You may have to order a few thousand dollars in merchandise you might otherwise not buy, but you add to a reputation that may be worth hundreds of thousands of dollars in the future.

Buying Situation Two: *Purchasing a Product You Know You Can Sell*

In many businesses, products for which there is more demand than supply are a rarity. Day-to-day profits depend on stocking merchandise (or selling services) for which there is an established, steady market. These products provide the cash flow that is the lifeblood of most companies.

However, if you can't buy these products at the right price, that lifeblood seeps away a little at a time until your profits are anemic. Let me give you an example. I have been negotiating with the manufacturer of a novelty product that has continued to sell very well over the last two years despite the depressed economy. I would very much like to sell this product, and I know my sales force could turn the merchandise over quickly. But to date, the supplier has only offered to sell me the product at a 25 percent discount from wholesale. I pay my salespeople a 15 percent commission, leaving 10 percent for me. At first glance, you might say that 10 percent on a product that I'm sure I can sell can help my cash flow and pay part of my overhead. However, purchasing the product ties up capital—even with today's low interest rates, that could cost me 2 percent. Shipping, marketing, warehousing, and other costs specifically related to that merchandise also eat up a few percentage points. The bottom line is that taking on the merchandise at that price could lose me substantial money, not to mention tying up capital and time I could be devoting to more profitable products. What looks like an adequate deal at first becomes, in fact, the first step toward financial instability.

In this situation, patience and discipline are required if you want to avoid the temptation of making a bad deal. The most effective strategy that will get you the product is the same as the one you used in Situation One: selling your character and your dedication to the product. The supplier of a successful product has no lack of customers. Ultimately, many of them will not perform to the suppliers satisfaction. Some will not meet payment terms, some will cancel orders, others will not move merchandise quickly enough. Your persistence in keeping negotiations open and constant emphasis on your high business standards will look increasingly attractive.

I've worked on suppliers for more than a year before we could arrive at a mutually satisfying arrangement. I can assure you the profits are worth the wait.

Buying Situation Three: *The Product Looks Attractive but Has No Proven Market*

By Situation Three, the pendulum has begun to swing in the opposite direction—the supplier wants to make the sale more than you want to buy. Let me explain with another example. Recently, I received a new line of girls' hair accessories. I thought they were well designed, well made, and attractive. The catalog was slick and well-done, as was the sales material. I could see myself carrying the line—but I could just as easily pass on it.

The crucial difference to me would be price. The price quoted in the solicitation was too high for me to consider—but then, most "sticker" prices are. Anyone who pays sticker price, whether it's on a car, a house, or a lot of merchandise, is giving his or her money away. For me to invest my time and money on an unproven product, I would have to get a real deal.

And I'm never afraid to ask. Remember my principle: "Have no shame." If you can't take the answer no, than you have a serious, perhaps fatal, business problem. Your strategy should be to come in with an initial offer that is very low.

However, it is crucial that you make your offer in a way that doesn't insult the seller. An arrogant or abrupt manner will kill any chance of negotiating. So will disparaging remarks about the product or its chances of succeeding in the marketplace. You'll keep the lines of negotiation open if you begin by saying, "I think you've got a very fine new line that may well succeed, but, unfortunately, I don't think I can afford to carry it unless I can buy from you at a price of _____." In this way, you don't make the quality of their product or its sales potential the issue in the negotiations. Rather, the issue becomes your personal guidelines on which products you can profitably carry and which products you can't. Then the supplier's only course of action—if he wants to make a sale—is to lower the price.

Again, patience and discipline are the keys to successful buying in this situation. You may end up having to compromise, but the compromise should be on the low end of the scale, not the high end. An argument that the supplier's profit margin would be too low should not sway you. He can make it up by taking a bigger margin on a sale to someone else who doesn't have your discipline.

What you can't expect, however, is for someone to sell you something for $1.50 that costs $2.00. Any successful long-term business relationship involves symbiosis—if one of you is going to succeed, you both have to succeed. You should realize that the seller needs to accumulate capital to continue to turn out product. You have to walk the line between being tough and being brutal.

Buying Situation Four: *The Seller Is Desperate*

This situation is the opposite of Situation One, because you hold all the cards. Price, rather than the qualities of the merchandise, becomes the major issue in the negotiation. I know that I can sell almost any type of merchandise if the price is low enough. When a supplier is obviously desperate to sell, I move quickly to get the price to the rock-bottom level.

You should, however, exercise some responsibility in your negotiations. The company that is desperate to unload merchandise today might develop products that you will want desperately at some point in the future. Conducting the present negotiations in any way that is insulting or demeaning is unwise and unethical. So is insisting on a deal that goes beyond a real bargain to the point of being brutal or unfair. Because your reputation—your character—is such a valuable asset (as we've emphasized above), any action that might tarnish you isn't worth a few extra dollars you could make applying pressure in a situation in which you hold all the cards. Again, patience and discipline will pay off in the long run.

Using the strategies described for these four situations will give you the confidence and flexibility necessary to sell the products successfully. Negotiating as a seller means assessing the situation in which your buyer finds himself, and acting appropriately. For example, if you have merchandise which is in hot demand, you're going to concentrate on the character of the buyer and his dedication to the product. On the other hand, if you have a new product that places the buyer in Situation Three, you know that price is the primary issue and that your best chance of making a deal at an adequate profit will require patience and discipline.

However, to repeat our main point once again, the greatest salesperson in the world can't make money selling something that cost him too much in the first place. Concentrate on buying skillfully, and you'll prosper. Sometimes the best deal turns out to be the one you never made.

Some Things to Think About

- View every purchase as a negotiation. While you can't bargain at the grocery store or the gas station, you can obtain some price concession in an amazing variety of other situations. Make a practice of offering a lower price, and keep a written record of how much money you save.

- In every negotiation, figure out the lowest initial offer you're comfortable with. Then offer at least 10 percent lower. You'll be surprised at the savings.

- Exercise patience and discipline by stretching out negotiations, even when you've made up your mind to buy. Walking away when the seller thinks you're hooked can win you additional concessions on your return visit.

Pick a Mentor
The Best Education You Can Get Is an M.B.A.—Master Businessperson Appreciator

> The greatest obstacle to discovery is not ignorance—
> it is the illusion of knowledge.
> —Daniel J. Boorstin

Recently, I read a report comparing education in the United States with that of the six other leading industrial nations. America ranked first, by a considerable margin, in the percentage of adults who had graduated from high school and in the percentage of adults who had graduated from college. Sounds good—until you read on to discover that American adults ranked dead last in actual knowledge of subjects from math to science to geography. In other words, we lead the world in diplomas on the wall. But far too often those diplomas are just pieces of paper.

The difference between our educational system and that in European countries was brought home to me at the high school graduation of someone we'll call Carl Smith. After the elaborate ceremony, we went back to the graduate's house for a big party. The Smiths ran a bed-and-breakfast in their home, and one of the guests at the party was a twenty-seven-year-old Dutch woman staying with them on her first U.S. visit. As I talked with her, I discovered that the graduation hoopla absolutely astounded her. She told me that in Holland, graduation ceremonies are unknown and the act of receiving a diploma has no special significance. The emphasis of the educational system isn't on obtaining a piece of paper, but on preparing students for a career or for higher education. Perhaps their concentration on what they are learning is one reason that Dutch students—and Dutch adults—put Americans to shame on standardized tests.

What do our high school and college diplomas really mean? They're primarily tickets that allow us to enter competition for certain jobs or competition for admission to another school. Some diplomas are won through diligence and hard work. Others, probably the majority, are gained by merely punching a time clock, doing the minimum to get by until the requirements for issuing the piece of paper are met.

If you think I'm being harsh, consider the following statistics. In 1971, when the Army was considerably swollen by Vietnam-era draftees, approximately 41 percent of enlisted men entering the service did not have high school diplomas. Of these, approximately one-quarter had achievement scores placing them at a fifth-grade level or below. For these men, the Army offered six-week courses designed to help non-high-school graduates prepare for the standardized test one needs to pass to get a high school equivalency diploma.

The results: More than 90 percent of those taking these six-week reviews of basic English, math, and other subjects earned high school equivalency diplomas. This included those soldiers who began at an educational level measured at fifth grade or below. These men and women attained scores on other standardized tests roughly equivalent to those attained by enlisted personnel who had graduated from regular high schools. This all sounds great—until you realize that the standards for issuing a high school equivalency diploma are math and reading skills that should be mastered at somewhere around an eighth- or ninth-grade level. What the high school equivalency program did was raise non-graduating soldiers to the mediocre level of soldiers who had earned that piece of paper certifying they were high school graduates.

In my mind, college diplomas don't mean a whole lot more. I recently saw a catalog from a state college that listed World Literature, a requirement for graduation, as a one-semester course that had a reading list of exactly five full books. With those standards, what does a diploma from that university really signify? And with studies that show 90 percent of American college students admit to having cheated, what is really the worth of any degree?

What is the point of my rather pointed attack on our educational system? What does it mean to you and me? Simply this: None of us are as smart as we think we are. I have earned a B.A. from Northeastern University, an institution with an excellent reputation. But I never would have gotten anywhere in business if I had the attitude that my need for education ended the day I was handed my sheepskin.

My degree was in psychology and, as I have explained previously, it was a ticket to a job with a consulting firm. But once I left that job and began my own business, the value of my "ticket" dropped to zero. Of course, I still had the knowledge that I'd gained in my studies. But I realized that my diploma itself couldn't earn me one more dollar in sales, gain me one more customer, or add a single item of merchandise to my line. I knew that to succeed, I had to find a way to go back to school, to acquire the skills I would need to make it in the real world.

It took me awhile to decide what to do. In the meantime, I relied on the work habits and techniques I'd picked up while dealing with people in all those years of driving around with my father. I soon discovered that those work habits and techniques gave me a solid foundation. That's when I realized that what I really needed to be was an M.B.A.—a Master Businessperson Appreciator. To get my degree in psychology, I had studied the wisdom and discoveries of the great figures in psychology from Sigmund Freud to B. F. Skinner. To become a master businessman myself, I had to acquire the wisdom and discoveries of the very best people in my business. I had to treat every contact I made not only as a potential sale, but as a learning experience.

That was easier said than done. I'm a talker. I'm brash and ambitious. When I meet someone, I want to make a good impression, then make sure the person realizes that I'm intelligent and eager to do business. In pursuit of these goals, I had the tendency to dominate conversations.

But over the course of years, I came to realize that I wasn't learning anything when I was talking. The more I listened, the more I absorbed and, curiously enough, the better impression I

made. I discovered that I was most effective when I used the
following techniques of a student:

- Listening intently and taking copious notes.
- Asking questions instead of making statements.
- Treating the person I was talking to with deference and
  respect.
- Studying my notes to extract the key points that will
  enhance my overall knowledge of the subject.

With the world as my new classroom, my sales at least doubled
every year for many years. So did my reputation for being a
smart, shrewd businessman. The respect I gained had absolutely
nothing to do with any diplomas hanging on my walls. Instead, it
had to do with the knowledge I demonstrated every day.

My attitude also contributed to the enjoyment I got out of my
daily activities. Cold sales calls weren't just a boring, intimidating
routine, but a chance to learn something new. Even if I didn't
write orders, my day wasn't wasted. Taking notes and studying
what I learned provided a sense of satisfaction in themselves that
seldom made me conclude that a day had been unproductive.

My attitude was so positive, I was so eager, that I often got a
chance to spend significant time with businesspeople who almost
never took unsolicited calls. People love to expound on what they
know. Answering questions makes them feel smarter and more
powerful. They came to associate those positive feelings with
talking to me, which made my telephone calls and visits far more
welcome.

This technique of getting ahead by learning from others isn't
my own discovery. Sam Walton applied the exact same technique
to building his family fortune, which is now estimated at more
than $23 billion. In his autobiography, *Made in America*, Walton
proudly claims that he visited more retail stores than anyone else
ever has. He just as proudly admits that the purpose of those visits
was to borrow every good idea, no matter how insignificant, that
he observed. His techniques were the same as mine—he asked a
lot of questions, listened intently, treated everyone with respect,
and took voluminous notes. In the beginning, those notes were
handwritten. Later, he carried a pocket tape recorder that he

used so frequently people joked that it had been grafted to his left hand. Every single week, Walton analyzed what he had learned and transmitted it to his key executives in Wal-Mart's weekly Saturday morning company meetings. Walton insisted that his employees learn from others, too, and be prepared to share their insights. It's no wonder that Wal-Mart is the number-one retailer in the United States—they've incorporated all the best ideas from all the other top retailers in the country.

The techniques the Japanese have used to become one of the two great economic powers in the world are another example of the importance of being an M.B.A. Busloads of Japanese businessmen snapping hundreds of pictures and taking notes as they tour factories have become such a common sight that it's become the fodder for jokes. But their skill at distilling and adopting the best ideas, techniques, and products we have to offer is no joking matter. The Japanese, and businesspeople in other countries in the Far East, seldom let their egos get in the way of seeking out new ideas and new ways of doing things so they can adapt them to their own use.

This attitude is in stark contrast to that of far too many American businesspeople who are too self-satisfied or too proud to admit that their ways of doing things may not always be the best. They seem to believe that a diploma on the wall and a title on the door mean that they've been anointed with a special intelligence. Their approach to new people and new situations is primarily "Let me tell you what I know" rather than "Let me find out what I can learn from you." Creativity, productivity, and profitability are the casualties.

There is no situation in which learning from others is more crucial than in mid-life career changes. The learning curve that exists when starting a career right out of school grows sharply steeper when you start a new career after a decade or more in the workplace, for two reasons. First, your internal expectations of success are higher. You simply won't be content with climbing slowly up the ladder, and if you don't take short cuts, your frustration level will become intolerable.

Second, you'll be held to higher standards by others inside and outside your new profession because you're not a kid. The situation in business is similar to the different ways a baseball team judges a twenty-three-year-old rookie pitcher and a thirty-five-year-old journeyman. The rookie will be given a year or two to prove himself, while even a few bad games can end the journeyman's stay with the club.

I don't present these negatives to discourage you from mid-life career changes—on the contrary, I'm so enthusiastic about them that I devote an entire chapter to the subject later in this book. I simply mention them because both can be overcome by shrewdly learning from others. People just out of school think they know everything. You're experienced enough in the world to realize that people who've spent twenty years in a business know more than you. The more you use your people skills to become friends with these people and pick their brains, the faster you'll advance.

Picking mentors has been absolutely crucial to my success in broadcasting. In less than two years, I went from being a total amateur to being part of the broadcast teams for a number of prestigious sporting events. I did it by straightforwardly and shamelessly learning from everyone I came in contact with, from on-air personalities to producers to engineers. It didn't matter that some of these people were considerably younger than I was—if they had something to teach, I was available and grateful to learn from them.

Learning even involved volunteering for jobs that could be considered gofer positions. Some of my friends thought that Stu Taylor, founder and president of a large, thriving national company, had lost his mind when he spent weekends lining up interviews, lugging equipment, and even fetching coffee and donuts while others handled the on-air chores at major sporting events. These friends were noticeably silent a year later when I was heard in dozens of countries broadcasting these same events.

These friends of mine didn't understand that I considered my volunteer duties a privilege and an honor, not demeaning tasks. I knew that I would learn more and make more contacts in one weekend at the Baseball Hall of Fame ceremonies than I could in years of schooling. Simply being part of a press conference and watching experienced reporters pose and follow up on questions provided a graduate-level-course worth of experience.

I recommend that everyone pick mentors. Notice the plural. I have never met an individual person who had such a commanding mastery of any field that he or she could serve as the only valuable source of inspiration. Rather, I have learned from dozens of mentors, drawing out people in conversation, observing them at work, and eliciting any kernels of knowledge they have. It works—and I'm living proof.

Some Things to Think About

- Make a list of all the people you admire in your field. Try to make contact with one of them each week, and interview that person as if you were a reporter for a trade publication. You'll find most people love to expound on what they do, and you'll be surprised at what you learn.

- Fight against jealousy. The reaction most of us experience when a competitor wins a big contract or a coworker snags a big promotion is anger. That anger, while unavoidable, is unproductive. Squelch your jealousy by studying that competitor or co-worker to find out why this battle was won—so you'll win the next one.

- Keep a pocket tape recorder handy. While you're driving, think about the appointment you just left or the person you last worked with. If you remember anything you could learn from them, make a note using the recorder.

It's Not Only What You Know

The Art and Science of Establishing Connections to Build a Highway to Success

> The greatest obstacle to success is the inability to turn to a friend and say one simple word: *Help.*
>
> —Winston Simold

When you read the title and subtitle above, you probably asked yourself, "Didn't Stu cover networking somewhere else in this book?" The answer, of course, is yes—my Sixth Principle, "Business Is a Contact Sport," describes the value of meeting as many people as possible in order to build a reliable information network. As I've emphasized before, reliable information is vital to keeping any business current and profitable.

But information isn't everything. If it were, then journalists and gossip columnists would run the world. Rather, it's only the starting point from which you have to develop a plan for reaching your goal.

Let me explain. Suppose you had some friends, amateur mountain climbers, who were vacationing in the Himalayas when they came across a rich vein of gold in a high, remote valley in Nepal. Because you are brilliant at cultivating contacts, your friends call you with the information first. But how much money does that call make you? That's right, the call alone makes you no money at all.

Before you can actually use that gold to make a profit, you've got to turn the information from the phone call into an infrastructure. You have to build a road from the base of the mountain to the valley; you have to build housing for your workers and build another road to get them to the mine; you have to build a road from the base of the mountain to the plant that will process the ore; and, finally, you have to find a way to build a road to market.

I use the word *road* because it is a perfect metaphor when talking about personal and professional success. Transportation has always been the key to building a profitable business or a profitable economy. History shows us those civilizations with access to transportation were the ones that flourished. The captains of industry in nineteenth-century America knew it when they built the transcontinental railroad, and the U.S. government knew it when it funded and built the interstate highway system after World War II.

When we set personal goals, our tendency is to daydream about transporting ourselves from where we are to where we want to be by mentally flying over the many miles and many obstacles in between. But a few major goals in life worth reaching are achieved so easily. Most require the painstaking process of surveying the land to find the best course, obtaining the proper equipment, laying down a solid foundation, then paving the way step by step. And if we do a good job, we have something permanent and long-lasting when we're done.

Our relationships with people are the "equipment" we use to achieve our goals; the "cement" is mutual consideration and trust. Both are essential to long-term planning and long-term success.

For an example of what I mean, let's go back in time to the period after my success with *Saturday Night Fever*. Snaring the national distribution rights to the movie posters gave me the opportunity to become a national distributor of fad merchandise. Using these rights and my information network, I was able to line up sales representatives all over the country to sell not only *Saturday Night Fever* posters, but my entire line of merchandise. Practically overnight, I had managed to take a giant step forward that would otherwise have taken me years.

But I knew that I hadn't really achieved my goal of establishing a sales network that would endure for years. The *Saturday Night Fever* fad was only the beginning of my relationship with my new sales representatives and thousands of new customers. If I didn't cement those relationships by continuing to provide profitable merchandise and top-quality service, I would have lost those representatives and those customers shortly after the demand for John Travolta posters faded.

As hard as I worked to meet demand during the raging fad, I worked harder after it was over. Every subsequent conversation, product introduction, and sales order was an opportunity for me to build solidly on the foundation that I had laid down. As the years passed, the "temporary road" that had been quickly built in a few days became a paved highway that allowed me to sell millions of dollars of merchandise over the next two decades.

I was very fortunate to get one big break that gave me a giant step toward my goal. Most of the time, your goal will seem as unreachable at first as that vein of gold high up in the remote Himalayan mountains. But if you think of success not as capturing lightning in a bottle, but as carefully laying the foundation for a permanent highway, you'll be more patient in achieving success through small steps.

Through a friend I heard of a remarkable man whose story is a textbook example of how making connections and cementing relationships can lead to achieving what seems like an impossible dream. This man I'll call Bill grew up in a struggling single-parent family in Milwaukee, Wisconsin. His mother worked for many years in one of the famous beer factories in that city, but when he was sixteen, her plant was shut down. Bill had to leave school in his junior year and go to work.

So far, this sounds like thousands of other stories you've heard. But Bill had dreams and a lot of ambition. Having seen firsthand the bitterness and despair his mother had suffered when she lost her job after eighteen years of hard work, he was determined to own his own business. And having grown up in an area where a new automobile was a prized status symbol, he was determined that business would be an automobile dealership.

So Bill decided to turn necessity—dropping out of school and finding a job—into an opportunity. After weeks of searching, he found a job as a delivery driver for an auto parts store. His customers were local service stations, and his first connections were the owners of those stations. Bill decided to provide them with the best and quickest service he could, going out of his way to correct problems or lend a helping hand. After a while, he discovered which of his customers were the best and most honest businessmen, and he began to pick their brains about every aspect of their businesses. Flattered, these men encouraged Bill to stop by in his spare time to share their experiences in servicing different types of automobiles and dealing with different types of people.

Finally, Bill got to be so close with one service station owner that he shared his dream of owning an automobile dealership. This man was so impressed with Bill's ambition and dedication that he used one of his connections to get Bill a job as a parts delivery driver for a large Ford dealership. Bill was so delighted that he not only did his job, but pitched in to help everyone else. Helpful and cheerful, he was well-liked, so no one minded if he asked questions about their work.

Soon Bill became especially interested in used cars. Like many dealerships, the one he worked for kept certain desirable trade-ins to sell on their own lot and shipped out the rest to wholesalers. Bill set about learning what specific qualities made the difference between selling a used car profitably and selling one unprofitably. Finally, after a year of learning, he decided to dabble in the business himself. He searched want ads and inspected a lot of used cars until he found one with a price and condition that met his criteria. He purchased the necessary parts for the car wholesale and had his friend the service station owner do the repairs. Holding his breath, he advertised the car. Two days later, he sold it for a one-thousand-dollar profit.

After a couple more profitable sales, Bill was able to purchase two cars at the same time, then three, then four. Word of mouth kept his phone ringing at home—he couldn't keep up with demand. That's when another connection led to another giant step. One of the dealership's top salespeople had been increasingly dissatisfied with the way he was being treated by the ownership. He suggested to Bill that the two of them become partners and open a used car lot. With some capital to invest, Bill jumped at the chance.

From this point on, Bill's drive for success shifted into a higher gear. He insisted that every customer be treated as if he or she were the most important person in the world. He offered an unconditional thirty-day money-back guarantee and free towing if the car broke down. Soon he and his partner were so busy that their major problem was keeping a supply of quality cars to sell.

Three years later, the two men who owned the Ford dealership Bill used to work for ran into serious financial problems. To the astonishment of Bill and his partner, the regional dealer-liaison manager for Ford approached them about purchasing the ailing dealership. Bill's reputation and the superior cash flow of his used car operation resulted in quick approval of the financing by a local bank.

At age twenty-seven, despite being a high school dropout, Bill achieved his dream of owning an automobile dealership. Today, twenty years later, he is one of the wealthiest and most admired men in the state. His success resulted primarily from his appreciation of the importance of making and cementing connections in pursuit of his goal.

Bill's story is fresh in my mind because I often thought about him when I decided that I wanted to become a radio talk show host. I had accumulated a lot more education, assets, and credentials than a sixteen-year-old high school dropout. Unfortunately, none of these things gave me any particular advantage in one of America's most competitive fields. There are more than ten thousand radio stations in the United States, all of which employ several experienced broadcasters eager for national exposure. Hundreds of retiring professional athletes look for broadcasting jobs every year. Each year top media schools such as Northwestern and Syracuse graduate some of the brightest and most talented communications students in the country.

My only important asset was my connections. Through a friend, I met a man who operated a national sports broadcasting network. He was having some marketing and administrative problems, and his cash flow prevented him from calling in high-priced consultants. We had dinner one night, and he asked for my help. I knew it would mean a considerable commitment of time, time that I would have to take away from my own business. But I also recognized that I was taking a step toward my goal. So I volunteered to help him.

A few months later, my friend needed someone to step in to fill in on a one-hour late-night talk show for one night. He asked if I'd be interested. I was extremely flattered and accepted. Another connection had been made.

The next step was turning a chance into a career. I prepared myself the best I could and went on the air. Evidently, I did well enough to be asked back for a second week, then a third. The door was opening wider.

But I still realized how fragile my toehold was. I went out of my way to cement any connections I could that might advance my career. I got to know everyone else at the network from engineers to producers to on-air talent, and I asked for their frank criticism and advice. I played tapes for my family and friends, seeking their criticism. And, most important, I cultivated my guests.

The key to attracting and keeping an audience is to book interesting, topical guests. Those of you who read the entertainment pages of the newspapers are no doubt familiar with the bloody and brutal war to win guests waged by the staffs of late night shows such as Jay Leno's "Tonight Show" and "Arsenio Hall." The battle to attract sports guests is less publicized, but no less intense. Added to my problems was that my show aired from 1:00 A.M. to 2:00 A.M., an extremely late hour to anyone on the East Coast who's not an insomniac.

My technique for overcoming the problem was to treat each guest not as a "one-night stand," but as a person with whom I wanted to develop a long-term relationship. In pursuing them I was polite, considerate, and patient. I prepared for every interview as if I were interviewing the President on network television, devouring books and newspaper clippings. Although some of my questions were tough, all of them were fair. In our call-in segments, I made sure that callers treated my guests with the same courtesy I did. And after the show, I expressed my thanks on the spot and followed up with more thanks later.

At first I didn't think I was doing anything different than any other talk show host. But I quickly developed contacts that I had never dreamed possible. I became friends with celebrities from basketball star Bill Walton to football greats Sam Huff and Jim Ringo to the fabulous boxer George Foreman.

My ability to attract top guests won me more hours on the air and better time slots. I became part of the broadcast team for such prestigious events as the Baseball Hall of Fame induction ceremonies and the NHL Stanley Cup Finals. And none of it would have happened if I hadn't been schooled in the art of making and cementing connections, building highways from where I am now to where I want to be in the future.

That's why I was dismayed when using and discarding people seemed to be the modus operandi of the 1980s. Obviously, I don't have the time or the energy to establish solid connections with everyone I meet. I have many acquaintances who I call occasionally to say hello and exchange information.

Some people may call this using people, but that couldn't be further from the truth. I give as much or more than I get. No matter how far I get down the road, I don't forget or neglect the people who helped me get started.

If you are just starting out, you should look at every person you meet as a potentially valuable asset. Cultivating and cementing those relationships can lead you closer to your goals.

Some Things to Think About

- At your local bookstore or your local library, pick up a copy of the autobiography of Sam Walton, founder of Wal-Mart. Walton got his start in a small town in Arkansas, a spot about as remote from the center of power in this country as our fabled gold mine in the Himalayas. The only way out of that town for Walton was "building roads" by establishing connections with people. Walton's first-person explanation is a textbook in the art of human relations.

- If you're having trouble finding a major goal in life, your range of acquaintances and experiences may be too limited. One solution is to volunteer your time for community service activities, from coaching youth sports to raising money for a local charity. I've made a lot of friends this way, and I've heard dozens of inspiring stories. You never know what chance meeting will turn into your first important connection.

- Reread Sam Walton's autobiography. You'll find something new to appreciate every time you do.

Beware of the Meeting Monster
How to Run a Successful Business Without Ever Scheduling a Meeting

> The smaller a man's ideas, the more words he uses to express them.
>
> —Henny Youngman

A very good friend of mine owns a chain of gift shops throughout New England, and the recent recession hit him hard. To save his business, he looked to every possible savings. He called me about a year ago to report that he'd just devoted two weeks to a detailed study of his company's telephone usage and was able to cut his costs by twenty-six thousand dollars a year.

I said, "I'll bet you a steak dinner that in two minutes I can save you ten times that amount of money."

He laughed. "Is this a joke?"

I said, "Do we have a bet?"

"Sure. What's the secret?"

I replied, "Cut out meetings."

He scoffed at me—until I faxed him a survey, conducted by a leading national consulting firm, which showed in detail how twelve thousand executives used their time. The results: On the average day, there were twelve million business meetings conducted in the United States. The executives spent an average of sixteen hours per week, or twenty-one weeks a year, in meetings. Executives paid $45,000 per year earned $18,500 for sitting in meetings. Those surveyed felt a third of those meetings were useless, as was a third of the time they spent in necessary meetings.

In my experience, those figures are way too low. I believe that 90 percent of all meetings are totally useless, resulting in a complete waste of time and of money. In most companies, meetings are a hidden monster that devours profits while sucking the confidence, creativity, and feelings of independence from the executives forced to endure them.

My friend wasn't convinced even after he read the study. But he was also desperate. We talked for a while, and I persuaded him to go cold turkey for one week. He sent a memo to all corporate and field staff canceling all scheduled meetings and banning the scheduling of new ones. The only consultations allowed were to cope with problems or emergencies.

There was a lot of grumbling from the staff, but the first result was that my friend had a lot of extra time on his hands. Starved for the feedback that he was used to getting from meetings, he spent two days on the road visiting his stores. He got many ideas to follow up on and discovered a few problems to solve, so he extended the meeting moratorium for another two weeks to free his time.

It's now almost a year later, and scheduled meetings are largely a thing of the past in my friend's company. He's trimmed his staff by 20 percent, closed four outlets, and opened two more. More impressively, the time he and his executives now have to work rather than talk has boosted sales 18 percent and produced a handsome operating profit at a time when his competitors are posting record losses.

I wasn't surprised, because I haven't scheduled a staff meeting in more than a decade. If you make a list of all the meetings you've attended, I bet you'll find the reason for the meeting fits under at least one of my Four Useless Reasons to Have Meetings:

Useless Reason One: *An Exercise of Management Power*

In feudal times, a lord exercised his power by having his vassals show up at the castle to kneel before him and describe how they'd contributed to his revenues. If the revenues weren't sufficient or the vassal unsuitably subservient, the lord would order him tossed in the dungeon or beheaded.

I've found many executives call meetings because they like to exercise their power over the schedules of their subordinates. They also revel in publicly handing out praise and criticism, rewards and punishments. I personally find such displays objectionable and, worse, counterproductive. I don't want people working for me who are motivated primarily by public praise or fear of public rebuke. I want self-starters who derive their satisfaction primarily from reaching their own goals. And I have absolutely no interest in calling a meeting to massage my own ego—I'd much rather have my employees caress the bottom line.

Useless Reason Two: *Pontificating*

How many people do you know whose one true romance is with the sound of their own voices? I know plenty. As a radio talk show host, I obviously love to speak to an audience. But, on the radio, I speak because I'm paid to speak. Calling a meeting to speak is preventing my employees from doing the jobs they're paid for.

Useless Reason Three: *Inability to Make a Decision*

Input from others is absolutely essential in the decision-making process, as I've discussed elsewhere in this book. In fact, I spend a good part of my day networking to obtain the widest possible input. But there comes a time when I have to evaluate that input and make my decision. But many executives can't or won't make a decision until it's been hashed and rehashed by a committee. This is terrible management for two reasons. First, if a manager has already made up his mind, he's calling a meeting simply to cover his rear end by being able to say, "Everyone else agreed with me." That makes the meeting a waste of everyone's time. If, on the other hand, the manager can't make the decision and has to rely on the input of others. That means he shouldn't be a manager in the first place.

Useless Reason Four: *Socializing*

If everyone in business took truth serum, you'd discover that a substantial percentage of all meetings are scheduled because the participants simply enjoy getting together to swap stories and generally socialize. With the recession putting intense pressure on most businesses these days, the desire to schedule an enjoyable respite is understandable.

But it's also expensive. Time wasted in meetings doesn't alleviate pressure, it eventually makes it worse, in the same way that putting off going to the dentist doesn't cure a toothache. The ultimate cure for pressure is to generate sales and lower costs to build profits. I've noticed that people working in thriving, profitable companies are a lot less tense than people working in struggling companies no matter how long they've been on the job.

Even if you understand my basic point, I'm sure you're now ready to present several very valid reasons to have meetings. Before you let me have it, I'd like to present my Five Meeting Alternatives that may forestall your objections.

Alternative One: *Be Accessible All the Time*

Remember some of the key principles I've already discussed: keep your door open, answer your own phone, read your mail. Accessibility encourages your employees to communicate with you when a problem or opportunity first arises instead of waiting until it reaches the crisis point. To use my dental metaphor again, if you brush and floss every day, you're far less likely to have emergencies.

Consistent communication is much more effective than occasional meetings. Much time at meetings is used providing background information and the history of a problem to bring everyone up to date. If you have any doubts, compare the time it takes to pick up the phone and answer a question to the time it takes to set up and conduct a meeting.

Alternative Two: *A Memo Is Worth a Thousand Words*

The act of putting our thoughts down in writing forces all of us to organize those thoughts much more effectively than we would if we just started talking about them. A telephone call to ask a question or discuss a problem is more effective than written communication. But for input that is relevant to a major decision, there is no substitute for writing. Nor is there a substitute for writing when presenting a major policy change or other important issue. Your employees may resent your request to put things in writing at first (you may not be fond of writing either), but it will ultimately save time and lead to better decisions.

Alternative Three: *Use Modern Information Technology*

When I walk into my local pharmacy to fill a prescription, my pharmacist enters my name and the medication into a computer, calling up information that includes other medications I'm taking, any allergies I may have had, complete instructions for taking the drug, and possible side effects. The time involved takes less than a minute, compared with the ten or twenty minutes it would have taken to look up physical records and consult books.

I was slow to appreciate the benefits of computers, but now I'm sold. I realize what a waste of time it was to have a sales manager come in to review sales figures or present an analysis of what those figures meant. Instead, with the computer, up-to-date information is at your fingertips and you can ask the software program to break down the information to answer almost all the questions you have. An electronic message center allows you to read notes or questions others have had about expense and revenue figures, eliminating your need to get together with them. With the cost of powerful personal computers plummeting, they can pay for themselves in months.

The fax machine is also a wonderful time saver. Sending documents, catalog pages, specifications for new products, or other information saves time and personal trips. For example, I have a friend who sells printing for a company in upstate New York. His two largest customers are located in the New York City area. He used to spend most of his time on the six hour drive back and forth, and the rest of it in meetings at both ends. The fax machine has cut the number of trips in half, and practically eliminated large meetings. When he's at the customer's headquarters, he faxes specifications, art, and other information to his plant, where production people have acted on it by the time he returns. When he's at the plant, he faxes finished art and samples of the final printed matter to the customer to obtain approvals over the phone. His effectiveness has doubled while his expenses have been cut in half.

Alternative Four: *A Picture Is Also Worth a Thousand Words*

Almost all publishing companies bring their salespeople together twice each year to hear editors make presentations about the books they will be selling in the next six months. The process is long and expensive. Now, at least one major publishing company videotapes the presentations of each editor and sends the completed tape to the salespeople well before the meeting. The salespeople review them at their leisure and organize their questions and comments. The meeting takes half the time, and the company also saves the expense of flying the editors to the meeting.

Creative use of videotape can serve numerous functions in the business world, many of which can drastically cut down on the necessity for meetings.

Alternative Five: *Socialize Outside of Business Hours*
I strongly believe that a company is strengthened when employees and managers get the chance to socialize, but I also strongly believe that such activity should take place outside of normal business hours. This way the camaraderie does not detract from building business or serving customers when they need us.

In Sam Walton's autobiography, *Made in America*, he emphasizes the importance of weekly company meetings in creating the enthusiasm and spirit that made Wal-Mart such an astounding success. But he also emphasizes that he insisted these meetings take place on Saturday mornings. Even though his wife, and many others, resented this commitment, Walton felt that extra special success required extra effort. Besides, during the week, he wanted his managers out in the field visiting stores, not sitting around at meetings.

Obviously, there are times when meetings cannot be avoided. But if you make a conscious effort to keep the meeting monster out of your business, that business will grow as never before.

Some Things to Think About

- Go over your appointment book for the last month and think about every meeting you attended. See how many of them fit my Four Useless Reasons to Have Meetings and how many could have been avoided using my Five Meeting Alternatives. The reasons for the few that remain are the only reasons to call meetings in the future.

- Become technologically literate. Add computer magazines and publications devoted to people who work at home to your browsing list. They contain information on products and services that can save time and money.

- Examine the way you make decisions. Learn to make them by yourself in a quiet place where others can't influence you. The only time decisions should be made at a meeting is when votes are necessary.

Be Market Smart
Using the Dynamics and Psychology of Impulse Buying

Lots of folks confuse bad management with destiny.
—Ken Hubbard

As I've said before, literally thousands of fad items have been submitted to me for my review over the last two decades. Virtually every person behind these items is convinced he or she has the next Pet Rock. These items range from mass-produced products that roll off assembly lines in giant Taiwanese factories to hand-crafted prototypes created in the basements and garages of aspiring entrepreneurs and inventors. How many of these products have become profitable, let alone household names? A small handful.

Inventors find these odds discouraging. You shouldn't. I certainly don't, because I've built a thriving business on selling that handful. You don't have to be a creative genius to become wealthy. Rather, you have to be what I call "market smart"; that is, you have to understand the dynamics and psychology that drive the impulse-buying market. In this chapter, I'm going to explain in detail what you need to know.

First, I'll repeat the distinction between a fad and a trend. A fad is a phenomenon that reaches masses of people and engages their attention and buying power for a brief period of time. Fads are phenomena that have no functional or practical value, and must be identifiable quickly, in a matter of seconds. A fad item's only value is the demand for it on any given day; a day later, if the demand slackens, that value is nothing.

When a fad dies, its death is generally sudden and permanent. Some fads that fit into this category are the Pet Rock, Deely

143

Bopper, Davy Crockett paraphernalia, and Khadaffi dart boards. Other fads have staying power and continue to sell year after year, such as the Slinky, Frisbee, and Super Ball.

A fad becomes a trend when it becomes part of pop culture. Some examples of fads that became trends are house plants, swimming pools, Reebok sneakers, and the Sony Walkman. Picking fads is dependent upon a combination of timing, luck, and psychology. The attention span of the American people shifts from one thing to another very quickly, and this behavior both creates fads and destroys them. Although there is conformity in people's pursuit of a fad, some fads thrive on consumers' urges to have their own identities. A prime example of this is the Cabbage Patch Doll, which people once went to bizarre extremes to purchase. Each doll had its own combination of looks, personality, and name; and these additional features served to enhance the saleability and individuality of the item. I had the short-lived good fortune to have sold baby clothing for the dolls to Cabbage Patch guru Xavier Roberts.

Many people make the mistake of creating or finding fads that are follow-ups to successful fads. This just never works and is a waste of time and money. For example, following the success of the Pet Rock, I was offered the Putchky Stone. I left this stone unturned, rejecting the product as I have so many others on the heels of a winner.

Modifying a successful fad—that is, taking a product that is successful in one mode and changing it to look slightly different in the search for a second fad—is also a mistake. Creating a duplicate of the original fad and manufacturing it into a different product most often meets with failure too.

I will use the successful 1989 Moonie as an example. Moonie was a doll people placed on the dashboard of a car. It dropped its pants when a rubber ball was squeezed. The Moonie doll was so successful that Moonie key chains were distributed the following year. True to form, they did not attain sales of any great magnitude.

The classic mistake occurs when manufacturers try to "milk" a product the second time around either by reintroducing it into the marketplace or presenting it in a new format. Some prime examples are the smile button, peace sign, and mood ring. Among the few notable exceptions are trolls.

I'm not saying nostalgia doesn't generate some sales, but it's just never the same the second time around. Unless there are some flea market operators around to take the dead goods off your hands, this marriage could be financially disastrous.

The other hazard is an attempt to bring back a personality or movie (with a spin-off) a second time. BuyRite, a company that produced Michael Jackson posters, buttons, and postcards to cash in big-time once, mistakenly went that route a second time in the late 1980s and bit the dust. Sequels to movies may be revenue enhancers as movies, but give me a sequel and I won't touch the spin-off merchandise. Of course, there are a few exceptions to all of this—my favorite fad-maker, John Travolta (who did it with *Saturday Night Fever*, *Grease*, and *Urban Cowboy*).

Another fad killer is the time-gapper. When two people are engaged in a tempestuous moment, do not douse them with ice water. When an impulse item is ringing up tremendous sales, don't pull the plug. Ken Framer's "Where's the Beef?" posters were the hottest commodity going in 1984 until Wendy's decided to pull the commercial for two months. The Simpsons entire product line was still in high gear when reruns of the show had to be broadcast because the twenty-three new animated half-hours were not ready when other prime-time shows premiered in September, 1990. When the new shows finally aired, consumer demand for Simpsons merchandise had waned.

There is a distinction between being a fad-maker and a fad-finder. My philosophy: The odds are a lot better of jumping on the coattails of a winner than of trying to create a fad on my own. There are so many thousands of gadgets, licensed spin-offs, ideas, and inventions that it is virtually impossible to come up with a monster fad. There are some individuals like Les Waggenheim of Leadworks (Gro-bots, Gro-beasts, printed pencils) and Dave Mac-Mahon (various electronic fads) who have either imported or manufactured major winners more than once, but by and large, my philosophy has always been to pursue the course of being a fad-finder; that is, recognizing the phenomenon of the day and promoting the hell out of it. Through this approach I've been able to experience fad heaven at least a hundred times.

Let's look at the risks involved in these two approaches. In general, the greater the risk, the greater the potential reward. Conversely, the greater the risk, the greater the potential loss. It's like making the decision to go with a money market account versus junk bonds. The safe route is to stay away from fads, but if the choice is to pursue the fad game, there are ways to minimize the risks without passing up the opportunity to cash in.

I almost never respond to the demands of manufacturers by committing to huge quantities from the beginning. I undoubtedly would have been forced out of business many years ago had I ordered in large quantities at the prodding of suppliers. It's just too risky. I say almost never, because it just doesn't make sense to tiptoe during the early stages of a fad's boom—that is, once you know the merchandise is blowing out of the stores. Some of the better examples of fads that were so hot immediately that caution wasn't necessary were merchandise off-shoots from Teenage Mutant Ninja Turtles and the early stages of "Beverly Hills 90210," O-ring bracelets, and printed shoelaces.

Several years ago Les Waggenheim was telling me about the terrific items he was having created in Japan. As he showed me around his Ohio headquarters, he pressured me in a good-natured way to order large quantities of what he thought were hot items. I backed off by testing small quantities of what, I must admit, looked to me to be potential winners. After Les tongue-in-cheek mocked me as a "jellyfish," I reminded him that as a manufacturer and contractor he *had* to order large quantities to defray fixed costs, such as molds, shipping, import duties, and sales. (By the way, Les also has had more than his share of losers.) But as a distributor I could play it safe, and if an item checked out, I could have it air-freighted in. I have the flexibility in my role of being able to move quickly to select an array of products, sometimes several per week. If one is successful I can make a commitment. If the item never takes off, I'm not locked into huge quantities. As a manufacturer, contractor, or licensee, there is more of a gamble because of the necessary investment of substantial money, time, and confidence into one or a few products before seeing how the market will react. And test marketing does not always work in the mercurial fad industry.

How do fads begin? Most people believe that they are deliberately created by entrepreneurs, citing the Hula Hoop, the Pet Rock (1983), and the Deely Bopper (1982). But fads can spring up in many different circumstances. Some are imported products: Mahjong, a parlor game, became the rage when introduced into the United States way back in the 1920s. Social issues can generate other fads—for example, "Peace," "Love," and "Ecology" in the early 1970s were the subjects of fad items, such as the famous posters and bumper stickers reading, "What if we had a war and nobody came?" Domestic and international politics can also be reflected in fad merchandise, from the Hitler voodoo doll that was popular in the 1940s, to Nixon/Agnew posters and bumper stickers, Ollie North merchandise, Khomeini and Khadaffi dart boards, and, as recently as the 1992 election, Clinton, Bush, and Perot dolls. The Persian Gulf War introduced hot sales of SAVE OUR FLAG buttons and decals, as well as of a large assortment of Saddam Hussein items.

Advertising campaigns can also create pop-culture fads, such as the California Raisins, Budweiser's Spuds Mackenzie, and the Hard Rock Cafe. Each of the first two examples demonstrates how TV commercials can play an unusual role not only in increasing product sales, but in spawning commercial spin-off successes in the process, which, in turn, add to additional product sales. Limited availability was the key factor in creating demand for Hard Rock Cafe T-shirts, which are only available through the clubs and are not sold through commercial outlets.

Fads are also "sexually transmitted," starting in the days of the Betty Grable pinups in the 1940s. The first recent sex-symbol poster success, with sales of about 7.5 million, was the Farrah Fawcett poster. Other successful fad posters have featured Cheryl Tiegs, Patty Hanson, and Bo Derek.

Can religion spawn a fad? Countless religious items appeared in stores everywhere when the Pope toured the United States in Fall of 1979. Many thousands of Pope posters were sold in just a short period of time, and Taylor Associates had the good fortune to sell our share.

TV personalities have produced many pop-culture fads, from the famous Fonz (Henry Winkler) from "Happy Days" (posters of the Fonz sold in millions) to Al Bundy of "Married with Children" to the biggest of all time, the cartoon characters, the Simpsons. The 1993 success story is Barney.

The music industry steadily gives birth to fads that have millions of fans seeking belts, caps, buttons, emblems, and posters with the pictures of rock personalities. The two premier music spin-off booms featured Michael Jackson and New Kids on the Block.

Some fads are fashion statements: hats, T-shirts, headbands, jewelry, sunglasses. Let's try some on for size: mood rings, O-rings, rubber sunglasses, Reebok sneakers, short-shorts, imprinted sweatpants, eyeglass holders . . . we could list hundreds of items in this category.

Movies? Two of the biggest: *Star Wars* and *E.T.* Other movies that have inspired successful commercial spin-offs include *Annie, Ghostbusters, Indiana Jones, Jaws, Rocky,* and *Who Framed Roger Rabbit?* Although the success of a movie does not guarantee the success of its spin-offs, any movie blockbuster has the potential to break out as a fad. However, a lot of people in my industry have gone broke betting that they could identify the ingredients in a movie that guaranteed strong merchandise sales. Movie tie-ins are among the riskiest of all fad merchandise.

News reporter David Wittman, previously of WBZ-TV in Boston, asked me during an interview if I could recall a movie failure that produced a merchandising bonanza. I couldn't. Success at the box office is essential for profitable merchandising—even though it doesn't guarantee profitable merchandising.

Sports licenses can be gold mines—as long as the franchise remains popular. Sport properties as fads generate a mega-million-dollar business with emphasis on baseball, football, hockey, basketball, and wrestling. Occasionally, popularity doesn't depend on a team's winning record—one of the greatest franchise sales for sports merchandise in history was for merchandise with the logo of the San Jose Sharks, an expansion hockey team.

You don't have to be a genius to determine what the hot fad is—people walking around wearing T-shirts, hats, and sneakers serve as human billboards. The trick to financial success is in anticipating what people are going to want. Sometimes this requires "gambling" on the outcome of a sports event. For example, I remember during the 1985–86 football season, when the New England Patriots won three consecutive playoff games, I signed up to distribute EASTERN DIVISION CHAMP shirts, and it was a harrowing experience. The shirts were marketable for only one week before each playoff. Shirts were to be produced for games with the New York Jets, the Raiders, and the Miami Dolphins (SQUISH THE FISH shirts). With each victory, merchandise had to be received by us the following day and shipped out that same day.

Prior to the 1986 Super Bowl confrontation with the Chicago

Bears, BURY THE BEARS T-shirts were a hot commodity. I was first in line to receive, at the crack of dawn the morning after the Patriot win, thousands of dozens of New England Patriot 1986 Super Bowl Champion T-shirts. KABOOM! Chicago Bears 46, New England Patriots 10. Disaster? Wrong! The shirts were only to be printed if the Patriots won. I made no upfront financial investment.

The exact same scenario unfolded for me during the 1986 World Series between the Boston Red Sox and the New York Mets. I was numero uno on the list to receive Boston Red Sox 1986 World Series "The Impossible Dream Come True" T-shirts autographed by the entire team, truly one of the most appealing shirts I have ever seen. Foiled again by the shocking Red Sox defeat, the shirts were never printed. Some other people who didn't understand the fad market and the unpredictability of sports weren't so fortunate. After two games, the Red Sox were up two to nothing in that Series. Based upon what appeared to be a Boston world championship team, a large concessionaire and baseball licensee in the Boston area committed an advance for scores of thousands of dollars on Red Sox World Series Champ hats and other paraphernalia to get the jump on the competition. They took a huge bath, stuck with worthless merchandise. Perhaps in a hundred years collectibles they might become, but I doubt any of us will be here to enjoy that reward.

Nobody knows what will surface as the next fad. It could be as sudden as the swell of patriotism after the beginning of the Persian Gulf War, or it could be as carefully orchestrated as the promotional campaign for a blockbuster movie. If you want to learn to take advantage of fads, you've got to learn to be a keen observer of social, cultural, and political trends. I've given you the basic information about the dynamics and psychology of impulse buying. What you need now is an "internship" of watching a few fads unfold and study the course of those fads carefully.

Some Things to Think About

- When you are debating becoming financially involved in a product, ask yourself if the product is a true fad. If public demand for the product isn't already strong, you're not investing, but gambling.

- Decide what category a fad product or line of merchandise fits into—movie spin-off, sports, etc. Compare the new product to successful fads in its field. If it doesn't meet all the criteria for success, stay away.

- The trickiest decision may come when deciding if a fad is going to disappear or become a trend. Fad sales plummet, while trends produce steady, consistent sales over a lengthy period of time.

Be a Business Masochist
If You Have to Beat Up on Somebody When a Mistake Is Made, Beat Up on Yourself

If you're going to do something wrong, at least enjoy it.
—Leo Rosten

Self-confidence is by far the most underrated quality in business. Certainly the stars of the business world—flamboyant corporate CEOs, high-powered attorneys, and Wall Street traders— demonstrate no shortage of ego. But it takes far more than a highly paid chief to run a profitable business. Rather, it's the overall quality of work by the collective employees of a company that is the main determinant of that company's success.

I've found that the highest quality of work is turned out by employees who do their jobs with confidence. From sales manager to shipping clerk, everyone should be able to concentrate their full energies on doing the jobs in front of them. Unfortunately, in many companies, thousands of hours are wasted by employees who are afraid of making a mistake, or who are brooding about punishment or criticism resulting from a past mistake. No company can aggressively seek profits and increase market share with defensive employees. Why are employees defensive? Because too many executives look for a scapegoat when something goes wrong.

It's easy to take out one's aggression and anger by beating up on someone else, so scapegoating is more the rule than the exception. The catharsis felt by executives is so pleasurable that they seldom stop to ponder what terrible damage to the corporation may result from their tantrums.

My philosophy couldn't be more different. In my company, I not only sign the paychecks, but I also take the heat. I call myself a business masochist—if I have to beat up on somebody when a mistake is made, I beat up on myself. It's not that I dwell on mistakes, rather, I want my employees to know that I realize perfection is impossible and that honest mistakes are an unavoidable part of doing business. I've found that employees who aren't afraid of mistakes end up making far fewer mistakes than tentative, defensive employees.

My philosophy doesn't extend to long-term laziness or incompetence—I occasionally have to let an employee go, just like anyone else. It doesn't mean that I don't call employees in to discuss mistakes and talk about how to avoid such mistakes in the future. But there's no retribution, no shouting, no blame. The reason: I spent years working for myself, a time when there was literally no one else to blame. I made plenty of mistakes and I got used to coping with them. The experience made me a better person and, I believe, a better employer.

One such mistake came following *Saturday Night Fever* and *Heaven Can Wait*. A friend of mine, Harvey Hutter, offered me the opportunity to distribute posters from the movie *Animal House*. To my regret, I rejected the offer—I wanted to latch on to another huge fad that would present an opportunity to inundate thousands of stores with merchandise on a nonguarantee, nonconsignment, nonexchange basis only. I didn't think *Animal House* would be big enough—and I was wrong.

I instead concentrated my attention on an offer of partial ownership of the poster license for Robert Stigwood's *Sergeant Pepper's Lonely Hearts Club Band* movie. Up until the time of *Saturday Night Fever*, the cost of licensing the rights to produce posters from a movie was no more than several thousand dollars. The *Sergeant Pepper* asking price was substantially more. I was tempted, but the deal fell through. In this case, I was lucky. The movie was a major failure and any associated merchandise would have been unsaleable.

My next opportunity was a project called the Music Box, a display unit that featured posters of pop and rock music celebrities such as Andy Gibb, Patti Smith, Dara Sedaka, Meatloaf, K. C. and the Sunshine Band, Bruce Springsteen, Hall and Oates, Sha–Na–Na, the Atlanta Rhythm Section, Captain Kool and the

Kings, the Bee Gees, and Paul Nicholas. I liked the concept so much that I invested capital. It was a brilliant idea, but perhaps ahead of its time. The day-to-day popularity swings in the music market made interest in the individual posters very uneven. Bruce Springsteen and Andy Gibb were very hot sellers, and Meatloaf and Patti Smith posters did moderately well. The rest were bombs. The results: When a twelve-dozen unit of posters was placed in a store, the sell-through was almost always less than 25 percent, a losing proposition.

That experience was bitter, but I learned from it. Placing greater quantities of the popular posters in fewer stores would have converted a loss into a substantial profit. I learned that the old saw that 20 percent of a sales line results in 80 percent of total sales was true. It makes sense in most cases to concentrate on fewer items for the 80 percent sales return. This will also reduce overhead and result overall in expedience, lower costs, and ease in operating the business.

It is always advisable to reduce risk as much as possible when vying for a property. As a rule of thumb, the degree of commitment should vary directly with the probability of success. In the case of *Saturday Night Fever, Heaven Can Wait,* and the Music Box, the potential rewards were enhanced by the degree of exclusivity. To this day I have no regrets about how I negotiated the deals.

The decidedly mixed market responses to musical and movie-related merchandise led me to lie low for a few years—until the success of Disney's *Who Framed Roger Rabbit?* indicated to me that sales of such merchandise were about to take off again. That's why when *Batman* came out and the media was filled with publicity generated by JCPenney's Batmania shops, Taco Bell giveaways, and the appearance of Batmobiles at local malls, I decided to act with assertiveness and plunge ahead.

Batmania kept my staff working nearly around the clock. I was totally involved, writing huge volumes of faxes and letters in between hundreds of telephone calls to buyers and suppliers. If my staff had been hesitant, if they had lacked self-confidence, if they had been afraid to make mistakes, the work never could have gotten done. But I could rely on them because they could rely on me to back them up.

Their responsibilities were awesome. They had to arrange for displays of merchandise to be exhibited at trade shows all over the country. They contacted suppliers and made arrangements for posters and buttons to arrive in prepackaged units, thus eliminating the cost of counting, assembly, and contract work (that is, rolling posters, putting them in plastic bags, and labeling them.) This meant when merchandise arrived at our location, employees just had to type orders, slap labels on boxes, and arrange for shipping.

Other products required more work. Squeeze bottles were packaged in 48-piece assortments and 144-piece displays— optimal selling units for retailers. Hair accessories and jewelry were prepacked so the retailer only had to open a box and remove the display. Our efficient in-house team was superbly skilled in handling the tidal wave of orders spawned by the craze, and each employee understood his or her function like a well-trained bomber pilot. This was a real team effort.

I recall one most amazing event during the height of this activity. My dear mother had passed away suddenly in October of 1988, and my father, who was suffering emotionally in the aftermath of having been happily married to her for fifty-four years, was spending many days with me on my business itinerary. During one of those wild and wooly mornings when my father was sitting in the office area apparently dozing comfortably, I was involved in a myriad of activities. When beckoned to take an overseas call, I referred the balance of an order waiting for pickup to someone in my office. During the transaction, an error in the amount of twelve hundred dollars was made in the customer's favor.

With phones ringing and people in the office, the customer left with his merchandise. Suddenly, my father awakened from his nap and commented that he thought a twelve-hundred-dollar mistake was made on a bill. Sure enough, the invoice proved him right. I will never comprehend how anyone could have grasped that. I was very proud to let him know of his contribution. He passed away a few months later, but I will always have the comfort of knowing he was able to share the *Batman* experience with me when he so desperately needed something to fill the void in his life.

However, the real point of this story from a management standpoint is that when the sizeable error was brought to my attention, I stepped in and took responsibility. My first thought was to not embarrass the employee who had made what was an unintentional mistake; a person who was working twelve hours per day under terrible pressure. Even if the error had not been reversable and had in fact cost me twelve hundred dollars, I still would have taken the responsibility. The reason: Demoralizing my staff, or even one employee, could have cost me tens of thousands of dollars at that time. Instead, calling my staff together for a moment to praise my father for catching "my" mistake reinforced the concept that all of us were part of a "family." Everyone worked even harder.

Taylor Associates attracted national media attention during this entire period in the form of newspaper, magazine, TV, and radio exposure, which proved to be better than any advertising we could have done. Although we had many international inquiries, legal restrictions prevented us from making overseas sales. We were besieged with complaints about black-market merchandise, but it never slowed our progress. While federal crackdowns were taking place, the demand for licensed merchandise increased. Our ability to finance the operation was greatly enhanced by all of the payments in advance we received and by C.O.D. shipments where credit was unacceptable or lacking. Even established accounts were complying with our request that they send up-front payments. This gave us the ability to pay our suppliers instantaneously. Although in most cases this was not requested, it allowed us to obtain, within reason, unlimited credit from suppliers who considered us a top priority account. Since 90–95 percent of those who ordered were certain to reorder, it became imperative for those credit limits in order to pay for merchandise. The period of concern is when a fad is near its end and accounts aren't likely to order. Throughout the endeavor we were very much in control of a situation that was out of control.

Organizing merchandise to be shipped and decentralizing the operation were difficult to implement since we could not afford the loss in time that coordinating the project would have required. My father always said, "Strike while the iron is hot; good things don't last." Fortunately for us, bad things didn't last either, as we overcame obstacle after obstacle.

While attention was focused on the movie blockbuster, our other fads were in full throttle. Friendship bracelets of many styles were popular and neon shoelaces had resurfaced. Our sales on the bracelets and shoelaces were prolific. In summary, the process of pursuing the full course of a fad is an exhausting one: identifying and qualifying the fad; selecting the item; setting the financial wheels in motion; negotiating the deal; obtaining the goods, and quantifying the amounts of merchandise to order; obtaining credit information; controlling the backorders; getting merchandise accumulated; providing a sales force with information; producing sales; watching cash flow; dealing with defective or return merchandise.

Remember, at the end of a fad, almost everyone wants to send back what is left in inventory. You now have to know when to cut back on ordering merchandise by keeping a keen eye on the rate of sales declines in the retail trade. Lastly, it's an art to get all of the money and make certain the profits aren't eaten up in uncollected debts and/or unsaleable inventory. Your merchandise can lose all of its value when the fad is over. The more stable the merchandise the more its value is retained.

The same is true of staff. Stability is the key and that comes from accepting the blame yourself and filling your people with the confidence to operate at maximum efficiency in a crisis.

Some Things to Think About

- Never criticize someone when you're angry—you'll never say the right thing. Worse, you may make inappropriate remarks that can ruin months, even years, of a good relationship.

- Get used to using the word *we* instead of *I* when talking about your business. If you need ego reinforcement, get it by looking at your balance sheet. Everyone you work with will double their efforts if they feel like an integral part of the team.

- If you make a mistake and lose your temper, apologize immediately and publicly. A private apology will never make up for a public humiliation. Saving face for your employees is much more important than saving face for yourself.

Put Yourself in the Spotlight
Cultivating Attention Can Make Your Reputation Grow

> There's no business like show business.
> —Irving Berlin

At the innocent age of fifteen, I decided to enter the world of business as a short-order cook at the now defunct Paragon Park—an amusement park abutting Nantasket Beach in Hull, Massachusetts. Professor of psychology, George Shanker—who spent the "off-season" educating students at NYU—welcomed me into the grand order of those who work directly with the masses. Slaving through sixty-hour work weeks for minimal wages, I endured my initiation into face-to-face consumer relations while applying Dr. Shanker's theories to the art of gourmet consumption, i.e., hot dogs, hamburgers, and pizza. Dr. Shanker's rhetoric was uncomplicated. "Give them something they like at a fair price and they'll come back." It was stimulus/response à la Pavlov and certainly a divergence from his clinical training. It was my first clue that there was an art to the seemingly simple act of selling to the public.

The following summer, after a successful freshman year in college, I graduated to the highly esteemed position of concession barker, which I was to hold for many summers to come. My older brother, Jason, had served a long stretch there, and I was destined to continue the tradition. During those teen years I began to sense that I had the instincts and the inclination to be a successful salesman.

It wasn't long after becoming a barker that I was elevated to the highest status job in the park—co-piloting the biggest money-making concession. As I explained earlier in this book, the cigarette/candy game consistently drew the biggest crowds and demanded a quick-witted gift of gab combined with the fast-hand reflexes of a gunfighter at the O.K. Corral. Not only was I blessed with both attributes, but I was also fortunate to be able to continue my education under the tutelage of the living legend of the booth, Harvey "The Ace" Goldberg—my senior by ten years.

I soon learned that successfully running that game wasn't a job, but a performance. If I do say so myself, the caliber of my performances ranked from terrific to virtuoso, attracting swarms of people—sometimes ten rows deep—to play the game. "Cigarettes, cigars, candy bars. Play dimes, quarters, halves and dollars. A dime gets you two packs, the quarter a half [carton of cigarettes], and a half [dollar] a carton." I was able to blend the art of fast-talking, a sense of humor, and an innate dexterity to operate the game. And it was all immense fun.

Because I was so young, I often had trouble determining what was "show business" and what was "showing off." On more than one occasion—because of my proclivity for immature pranks—I had to be reprimanded and "farmed out" to the less prestigious doll stands. My employer, Myron Klayman—who, some twenty-five years later, was to become my first sales manager—was always patient in reminding me that while he appreciated my caustic approach, dry sense of humor, and ability to draw large crowds, my primary function was to bring in money for the establishment. As in real estate, where the three most important criteria are location, location, and location; in business the bottom line is net profit, net profit, and net profit. I could be as flamboyant as I liked—as long as the net result was profits, not mischief.

My early success in the carnival led me to believe that I was as sharp as they come. Five years later, I got a painful lesson in how showmanship wasn't the only criterion for success when I met a first-rate schemer named Tony King. Tony told everyone that he was about to begin a business manufacturing disposable paper dresses. He incorporated under the name of The Paper Bag and peddled stock to a group of investors, including yours truly.

It turned out that the only thing that proved to be disposable was my one-thousand-dollar investment as well as the contributions to the "Tony King Fund" from other downtrodden speculators. One deal after another fizzled, meetings were canceled, and facts and figures did not seem to support the content of King's statements. I began to wonder about Mr. King's grandiose plans for expanding his bag line into disposable aprons, shirts, and anything else he could concoct. But before I completely wised up, Tony King simply exited, stage left. From that point on I meticulously investigated the credentials of anyone to whom I was to entrust money. I also pledged to myself that I would never make glib public promises that I couldn't keep.

As for my more formal education, my years at Northeastern University were highlighted by many rewarding undertakings. I had two fascinating research jobs at Sperry-Rand Corporation and the Harvard School of Public Health. On campus I served as president of the Psychology Society, played enough ping pong to become one of the college's top table tennis players, and received an unforgettable indoctrination into the entertainment business by managing several rock and roll groups.

One of my most memorable clients was Chuck Sims—a fabulous young black entertainer. We worked on a routine and some vocals, and before I knew it I was booking gigs. My standard emcee club introduction was: "Ladies and gentlemen, it gives me great pleasure at this time to introduce a young man from Birmingham, Alabama, who in just a short period of time has made a name for himself in the rhythm and blues and pop field. He's appeared on the Otis Redding tour and has sung with such other notable celebrities as Wilson Pickett and James Brown. How about a nice warm round of applause for Misterrrr Chuck Sims!" Chuck would make his entrance, we would do a little dance routine together, and then he would perform. Could he ever do a rendition of "In the Still of the Night"!

I continued this venture for about six months, but discovered the hardships of dealing with contract disputes, no-shows, and too many logistical problems required me to expend more time than I had. But while it lasted, there were lots of laughs. Several years later I re-entered the entertainment world as a producer for a Boston-based TV production "Stage Door Disco." After this, I briefly served as a writer for another Boston TV station.

We all undergo a spectrum of experiences that contributes to our overall base of learning. Usually a lesson in business, for example, comes from a direct business experience. In my case, however, I seem to have a particular affinity for devising business-lesson analogies from a wide variety of situations. One such experience—which illustrated how important preparedness can be—stemmed from athletics.

Throughout my high school and college days I was a devoted sports enthusiast and played a great deal of table tennis. My forte was a strong defense against the attacks of offense-oriented players. My modus operandi was simply to let them hammer away at me until their frustration inevitably did them in.

One day a good friend of mine, A.G., set me up for a multiple match. A.G.—who had at least eight pints of gambling blood in his body—thought he could make a fast dollar by bragging about my ping pong prowess and setting up matches on which he wagered. In this match he pitted me against four of Thailand's top players—Son Pon and three teammates. Although I took the game seriously, my approach was rather laid-back. A sweatshirt, jeans, a pair of sneakers, and challenging competition were all that was necessary for me to have fun. Son Pon and his buddies arrived for the match in a fancy sports car. They were clad from head to toe in table tennis combat gear.

I had never done any physical warm-up prior to a match. It therefore struck me as funny when my opponents went through twenty minutes of stretching exercises. By that time they had attracted a small crowd, which apparently gathered in anticipation of viewing my annihilation. The audience was almost like a group of people waiting for someone to leap from the ledge of a skyscraper. Had I been intimidated by all of this hoopla, I might have packed it in right then and there. But as cocky as it sounds, I just didn't believe I could be beaten.

In a meticulous manner I disposed of the Thailand Four, patiently outlasting each of them both mentally and physically. A.G. collected his money with an ear-to-ear grin on his face. Son Pon and his entourage left the scene gracious in defeat, but nonetheless a bit dazed.

I'm not saying everyone is going to win at everything they do. But, if a person exudes an image of self confidence, while being physically and mentally prepared for a challenge, he or she will not be beaten by intimidation. The same principle applies in any business.

I've found that my attitude has been particularly important in one area in which so many executives—and so many corporations—do such a terrible job. That area is dealing with the media. It puzzles me why otherwise confident, informative, capable businesspeople turn shy or paranoid at the mention of a newspaper or television interview. I've used the word *media* at meetings and parties, and from the reaction, you would have thought I'd said KGB or IRS.

As I've said, promoting yourself and your company is show business. I believe that mass media is by far the most effective and least expensive way to reach a large audience. Why in heaven's name would I fear anyone or any organization that could give me that kind of exposure?

The obvious answer is that any person or any organization that has something to hide, that's having a problem, or that is under attack is going to fear media contact. But if this response is logical, it would be equally logical to hide in our offices and avoid answering the phone when a customer has a problem. Running away from an internal or sales problem invariably makes the situation worse. So does running away from the media when a problem occurs.

A classic example of the wrong way to deal with the media occurred when the state of California announced that it has been investigating cases of phony repairs in Sears automotive centers in the state. Sears spokesmen responded by angrily attacking the state inspectors while top corporate officers made themselves unavailable. The result: No one knew for sure if Sears was guilty, but they sure acted guilty. The company suffered severe blows to its image and its business before it came to its senses and began dealing openly with the media.

Fortunately, few of us will have to deal with such terrible crises. We can concentrate instead on how to make ourselves "media darlings," using the media to enhance our personal and corporate reputations. How do we do that if we're not Madonna? The first step is understanding how the media operates. Most of the people quoted in newspapers and interviewed on television and radio every day are not celebrities. They are simply people who have something to say about a specific subject on which they have knowledge or experience.

I'll use myself as an example. My business is fads, and when a fad is hot, the media often focuses attention on it. To gain exposure for my company, all I have to do is let people know that I exist and that I'd be delighted to be interviewed. Many companies hire public relations firms or consultants to get that word out—you can do it yourself. When you read the paper, pay attention to what kind of news is carried in each section. Scan the radio dial to get a feel for which talk show hosts are interested in which subjects. Watch local TV news shows and get an idea of the way they cover stories.

Inevitably, your line of work will be of interest at some time of the year. I'll use some simple examples. If you plow snow, people will be interested in your experiences during a major snowstorm. If you own a restaurant near a defense-oriented manufacturer, you can discuss your views of how a new contract or new cutbacks will affect business in your area. If you own a toy store, you can talk about the best and worst buys for parents at Christmastime.

If you think you have something to contribute to a newspaper story or a broadcast show, don't be shy about making contact. I've seen high-powered salespeople who thrive on cold calls turn into lumps of Jell-O at the thought of walking into a TV station or newspaper office. Now that I'm a member of the media, I can personally tell you that every journalist is always looking for new ideas and new sources, just like I'm always available to look at new products for my fad business. If you treat dealing with the media like making any other sales call, you'll be treated extremely well.

Of course, the more you learn about how the media operates, the more effective you'll be. Calling a TV newsroom a half-hour before the six o'clock news or calling an editor a half-hour before deadline might well get you a rude response. I'd strongly recommend that every person in business take an evening adult education or college course in basic public relations.

I've found that it can pay off immensely. For example, being quoted in a *Newsweek* article about the *Batman* fad brought me new customers and enhanced by credibility with suppliers. In a number of instances, even a sparkling credit rating and an offer to pay for merchandise C.O.D. has failed to impress a licensee with a product in great demand. However, in most of those cases, copies of my press clippings, which proved I could command media attention, did the trick.

The bottom line is, you should treat your business more like show business. You don't have to be a polished talker or a celebrity. You should just be prepared to do your best while maintaining a strong positive attitude, and let the chips fall where they may. If you are knocked down—just like the song says—pick yourself up and start all over again. Be tenacious.

Some Things to Think About

- You don't have to be a mesmerizing public speaker to give a good interview. The key is practice. Pick sample topics, then have a friend interview you. Review audio or video tapes of the practice interviews. You'll be surprised how quickly you become proficient.

- Keep a file of news stories that relate to your industry. After a while, you will begin to get a sense of what kinds of information about that industry interest the press.

- If you are uncomfortable contacting the media directly, hire a public relations consultant. You will probably find that the exposure is well worth the expense.

Invest in Yourself
Good Reasons Why You Should Be Eager to Go Back to School

Have no fear of perfection; you'll never reach it.
—Salvador Dali

I've found that all of us who've attained some measure of success in this world unconsciously become know-it-alls. Give us a bit of relaxation and an audience, and most of us can and will wax eloquent about the nature of our businesses and the secrets of our success. It's unavoidable and—I must add—enjoyable.

The problem comes when we become know-it-alls on the job. Today, that attitude is deadly. As I've pointed out so many times, profound change regularly occurs almost overnight. Take the break-up of the Soviet Union. Can you name the twenty-three new republics? Can you give me a capsule view of each one's economic weaknesses and strengths? How about rating the potential markets? Or rating them as potential competitors for business in Western Europe?

I'd have a problem doing this, and I'll bet you would too. But managers in any business will find it profitable, and perhaps necessary, to know this information, so they have to "go back to school."

All of our schedules are so hectic, so packed with activities, that investing time just to learn about a new subject seems wasteful, a romantic fantasy. Yet it's the key to growth in these turbulent times.

Experts estimate that the knowledge graduating engineering students bring into the workplace will be largely obsolete less than five years from the date on which they receive their diplomas. If they don't keep up with advances in their fields, they will be as good as unemployable in their chosen profession. I'm not an engineer, but I have noticed that things change with lightning speed in my field too. In fact, they always have, since the beginning of my career. That's why I've made it a habit to invest time in educating myself. In this chapter, I'm going to show you what I mean.

As I've discussed before, my father made his living in the distressed-goods business. In other words, he bought merchandise such as discontinued products and overstocks. To be successful in that very difficult business, my father had to have two qualities. First, he had to have a working knowledge of a vast array of different fields. One day he might be buying candy; the next day, furniture; the third day, machine tools. When he found goods to buy, he didn't have the luxury of spending two weeks studying the market. He had to make an offer on the spot and live with the result.

Second, he had to be able to move with lightning speed. The moment he made a purchase, his cash was tied up in merchandise. Every day cost him money. Procrastination was fatal. If the best he could do with a lot was to sell it quickly at a small loss, he never hesitated. He knew that small loss would likely be a bigger loss the next day.

My father's experiences are extremely relevant today. Not because he was a good example of an entrepreneur, but because in many industries, new products turn into distressed goods almost from the moment they reach the market. If that sounds strange, consider the computer business. An acquaintance of mine who runs a small public relations firm bought a new IBM computer system five years ago at a cost of about five thousand dollars. Today, an identical system would cost him between three and four hundred dollars. That price drop after introduction is true of every single product put on the market since then.

The only way a computer company can continue making money is to consider every finished product obsolete, concentrating on selling it as quickly as possible while devoting intense time and energy to the development of a new level of technology. Some computer companies that have realized this are faring extremely well—Apple is a good example. Others, hampered by institutional bureaucracy, are struggling—take IBM, for example.

Electronics are another good example. Almost every piece of

electronic equipment, from color televisions to VCRs to compact disc players, is less expensive than it was five years ago. Again, the only way to compete is to treat every new product as distressed goods and move on to the new generation of technology.

A third, and a bit more recent example, is the automobile business. American auto companies, especially General Motors, have received the rude shock of learning that foreign companies can bring innovative products to the market much more quickly than they can. This means that a new General Motors car, in comparison to a new car from some other manufacturers, is in some respects already obsolete. This translates into severe economic problems.

After these three examples, you can see why I draw the comparison between my father's business and my business, the fad business. I could go on and on. There is absolutely no business today that can assume that the product it places on the shelves today will continue to be competitive for a year, much less ten years. Change can be absolutely deadly.

The key to managing change is education. My father was a pioneer in educating himself. When he stopped at a factory to inquire about distressed goods, he didn't turn around and walk out the door if there was nothing for him to buy. Instead, he stayed to ask questions. What were the company's products? Where did they get their raw materials? Who were their customers? Who was their competition? What new products were in the works?

Many times when I was traveling with my father, I grew impatient, silently criticizing him for being too social. Only later, when I went into business for myself, did I understand how shrewd he was. All those hours of conversation provided knowledge that was absolutely essential for him to stay in business.

I can guarantee it's absolutely essential for you, too. I've often talked in this book about the importance of keeping up with the newspapers, magazines, etc., in order to spot new fads. Here, I'm talking about an education process that includes formal classes. In the last chapter, I recommend taking a public relations course at a local college or adult education center. Unless you're so disciplined that you could complete a college-level course through self-study, I recommend taking classes, seminars, and other formal programs on a regular basis.

Today, a vast variety of programs are offered in nearly every location around the country. Just yesterday, an acquaintance of mine, who runs his own media consulting firm, called me to rave about a three-day seminar on cable TV programming and advertising that he attended in New York. Another friend took a data-processing seminar sponsored by a computer software manufacturer—he's already cut his inventory time by one-third. Another manufacturer I talked with is going to New York for a program on third-world markets sponsored by the U.S. Commerce Department.

These people aren't ashamed to consider themselves students—even though they are well into their forties and fifties. You shouldn't be either. If you think education is beneath you, consider that the most prestigious job in the United States involves, to a great extent, being the nation's number one student. That's right, the complexity and breadth of problems facing the president of the United States forces him to spend at least half of his time (according to one political scientist's estimate) "going to school." Since his inauguration, President Clinton has spent hours pouring over thick studies and sitting in at briefings. If it's essential for his job, it certainly is for yours and mine.

Some Things to Think About

- Take business seriously, but not so seriously that you can't see the humor in your daily activities. Humor is very important in coping with the pressures of any business.

- Every job opportunity should be a learning experience. Take a positive approach, even if you dislike the job. Concentrating on the positive will keep you functioning on a high level until you can find another job.

- Keep your nose to the grindstone. Hard work eventually pays dividends.

Stoke the Fires While They're Hot
The Essence of Business Genius

If I had known my son was going to be president of Bolivia, I would have taught him how to read and write.
— Enrique Peñaranda's mother

Business management today is dominated by M.B.A.'s from the nation's finest business schools. Their expertise, in certain areas, is invaluable—particularly when it involves integrating technology with traditional business structures and practices.

But M.B.A.'s can be incredibly stupid, too. I can't believe how many companies ignore the most fundamental element of business—when you've got a hot product, a strong consumer demand, a great service, you muster every resource to stoke the fires. You don't commission studies, call meetings, organize consumer focus groups—you pick up your corporate bugle and sound the cavalry charge.

Many huge businesses today remind me of a guy who purchases a winning lottery ticket and then neglects to pick up the money. Nothing is more important than cashing in when the moment is right.

Recent business history is full of examples of companies that have failed to take advantage of success. A current case study is troubled General Motors, the nation's largest auto company, teetering on the verge of financial disaster. The one bright spot for GM has been its Saturn division, in which a combination of innovative design, innovative labor relations, and innovative management has produced a product so hot that customers are waiting six weeks or more for their vehicles.

If you were running General Motors, wouldn't you move heaven and hell to reorganize all your other divisions to emulate the Saturn model? I know I would. But the entrenched bureaucracy of GM hasn't even begun to tackle that task. Indeed, muddled decision making has at times threatened to ruin even Saturn. The bottom line is that if GM goes under, the fault doesn't lie in Washington or Tokyo, but internally.

One of my strengths has been striking while the iron is hot—as you can see in the following three case studies:

The Ninja Turtle Phenomenon

During the 1970s, fads normally began in California and spread eastward across the country. In that period, fad merchandise tended to appear first in small individually owned stores before being picked up by major chains. In the 1980s, both patterns were reversed. One example of the change is the Teenage Mutant Ninja Turtle craze.

Although I had heard of Ninja Turtle comic books and Ninja Turtle toys prior to 1989, I knew that the market for these items was a small group of preteenage boys. Name recognition for the Turtles was probably no more than 5 to 8 percent of the population. Then, in late 1989 and early 1990, for some unfathomable reason, that recognition skyrocketed to close to 50 percent. Ninja Turtle mania was about to take place.

My first professional interest resulted from a conversation with the merchandise manager of a large retail chain store who informed me that Ninja Turtle toys and game sales were increasing at an accelerated pace. He told me I should watch them carefully. I witnessed isolated examples of interest spurts, but big things didn't really start to happen until the fall of 1989. Many people attributed the increase in attention to publicity surrounding the first Teenage Mutant Ninja Turtles movie, which was scheduled to open in March 1990. I, however, believed that toy sales were taking off in a groundswell of interest that had nothing to do with the movie. Few people had any idea that that movie would become one of the highest grossing films of all time, spurring merchandise sales that would surpass even *Batman*.

I was one of the first people to place substantial orders on Ninja Turtle T-shirts. I quickly added other Ninja Turtle items to enhance my line: hats, posters, aprons, stickers, squeeze bottles, and patches. They sold well, but the merchandise became even hotter when the movie opened.

I plunged in with my characteristic zeal. The fad has turned out to be very long-lived—indeed, sales of Ninja Turtle toys have become classic as opposed to fad items. For me, Ninja Turtles was the second most successful fad in my company's history.

Why did these unlikely creatures attain such popularity, joining the ranks of other classic merchandise booms like Garfield, Looney Tunes, Barbie, GI Joe, and Superman? I believe that the key was their appeal to preteen boys, who expressed delight in not having to share the enigma of their popularity with their parents and other adults. They fell in love with the bizarre heroes and the imaginary world in which they lived. I never understood the appeal, but I understood the power of their fans at the cash registers.

The Simpsons

Simpsons merchandise was the biggest all-time seller in the history of Taylor Associates. Although Ninja Turtle merchandise might eventually overtake it, to my great surprise Bart and his family have produced more revenue than even *Batman*.

I never had the opportunity to see the short Simpsons cartoons that aired on Fox's "Tracy Ullman Show." But evidently their mixture of "All in the Family" and "Married with Children" sparked interest in network executives. As the Simpsons became cult figures, Fox ordered production of a half-hour primetime cartoon, the first since "The Jetsons."

The fad literally began the morning after the first Simpsons show. I have never, ever seen anything like it. My phones literally exploded. Needless to say, I got the "message." The problem was how to get the product.

I immediately got on the phone and entered into negotiations for Simpsons T-shirts—although *negotiation* is not the right term to describe a situation in which the explosion in popularity had put the licensee in the driver's seat to dictate fixed terms and fixed prices. My posture ended up being a combination of financial incentives, cooperation, and a bit of plain, old-fashioned begging. My primary advantages were that I could order in huge quantities and that I would pay in full in advance. I didn't ask for any special accommodation on styles, colors, sizing, or packaging.

In this situation, many executives would over-negotiate to cover themselves with their superiors or try to prove that they were hard-nosed bargainers. Listen to Stu Taylor: Don't worry about image when you're sitting on top of a gold mine. All I wanted to do was get merchandise, and when I did, I quickly and politely got off the phone. Soon thousands of dozens of T-shirts were pouring in and out of my warehouse.

But I didn't stop with T-shirts. I shipped Simpsons hats, posters, squeeze bottles, bendables, earrings, and bumper stickers. The scene around our warehouse each day looked like out-takes from a Keystone Cops reel. The frenzy nearly did me and my employees in. But we all understood that gold mines aren't discovered every day. Each minute was precious. Even though I'm amazed at how we survived, we made a killing.

Curiously, this was one fad that was cooled not by a change in the public's interest, but by the network. If you remember, the Simpsons premiered as a summer replacement series, and nobody had any idea how successful the show would be. Because animated shows take time to produce, the network had run out of new episodes in September. They had to show reruns while others were being filmed. The reruns cooled interest in the merchandise. On the one hand, I was glad for the relief; on the other hand . . .

Dick Tracy

The pre-release promotion for *Dick Tracy* within the merchandising industry was intense. In November 1989, when I took my family to the MGM studios at Disney World, I began to relish the thought of profiting from *Dick Tracy* merchandise, even though the release date was seven months away. However, as the months passed, I was surprised by how little television advertising was done for the film. I'd never seen this combination of intense merchandising promotion coupled with a curious lack of promotion of the actual film. Perhaps this situation is one reason why the actual sales of merchandise did not live up to expectations.

But are we defining success by merchandise sold *into* the stores or by merchandise sold *out of* the stores? Many *Dick Tracy* sales exceeded all *Batman* sales in presales to the stores, but of course that is only part of the story. If it doesn't sell at retail level there is no repeat business for anyone.

Dick Tracy grossed over a hundred million dollars (not including the video) at the box office, but by *Batman* standards fell well over a hundred million dollars short.

People's expectations of a megahit by new definitions were dashed. On a merchandising level, my theory is that the bizarre makeup of Michael Keaton's and Jack Nicholson's characters mesmerized people and stimulated sales on merchandise. This attribute was missing with Warren Beatty's staid character. Even Madonna was not electrifying enough to overcome the obstacles. *Dick Tracy* also had to contend with a share of the market with Ninja Turtles, the Simpsons, and New Kids on the Block.

For all practical purposes, *Batman* represented a new high in frenzied buying after an extended down cycle in the fad business. *Batman* also enjoyed more than a half-year bonus period from merchandise sales and build-up, while *Dick Tracy* was basically at the mercy of the movie's opening for speculative buyers who wanted to witness the crowd reaction.

Movie-related merchandise has a short life and a complete death once the movie has run its course, and the movie *Dick Tracy* was at the mercy of this rolling of the dice. Nineteen-ninety normally would have been considered a banner year second to none had it not been compared to the record summer of 1989 with *Batman, Ghostbusters, Indiana Jones and the Last Crusade,* and *Back to the Future.* Most merchandise sales occurred prior to *Dick Tracy*'s opening, so the market was more saturated than it should have been, considering the ultimate level of the film's appeal and success.

Your reaction to these stories may be, "Well, putting forth full effort when a fad like the Simpsons is hot seems obvious." A lot of people would agree—in principle. But when it comes down to making that superior effort every day, day in and day out, most people fall short.

I'll give you another, more routine example. I have a friend who's in the wholesale gift and novelty business. A lot of his annual revenue comes from supplying merchandise priced at five dollars and under to PTAs and other nonprofit groups that run Christmas gift sales. You may not even know that such sales exist, but they're big business—an average three- or four-day PTA sale can generate three to five thousand dollars in sales, and my friend supplies over one hundred groups.

What's the catch? (There's always a catch in making a fortune.) The merchandise is supplied to the school and other groups on consignment. Whatever doesn't sell, my friend takes back. The financial health of his business depends on how well he judges what's going to sell and what's not going to sell.

My friend is good at what he does and he does pretty well. But one day I was visiting him in the middle of the school sale season and his phones were dead. I asked him why his people weren't on the phones finding out what was selling and what wasn't. He replied that everyone was so tired after packing up all the merchandise that they were taking a break before the returns came in.

After a long discussion, I persuaded him that he could double his net profit if he had an idea about what was hot among students and what wasn't. The next year, he actually visited the first sale of the season. To his surprise, he noted about eight products that were literally flying off the tables on which they were displayed. He rushed back to his office, got on the phone, and ordered huge quantities from his suppliers. He made a special effort to get the hot items into the hands of his other customers.

The results were dramatic. In one case, his Christmas sales on one item rose from one hundred dozen to nearly eight hundred dozen. My friend hasn't stopped thanking me since.

Long ago I made a pledge that I recommend to you. I stopped spending endless hours analyzing my business in an attempt to figure out why one item was selling like crazy while another equally attractive item (at least, equally attractive to me) sat on the shelves collecting dust. I finally decided the variables of consumer demand were beyond my analysis—and probably that of most other people. I decided to take the public's judgment at face value. I've never regretted my decision. You won't either.

Some Things to Think About

- Make note of how much time you spend selling each individual line or product. You probably spend twice the time on products that aren't moving as on products that are. Reverse the apportionment of time and bask in the profits.

- Become obsessed with visiting your competitors and noting what's selling. Sam Walton spent endless hours doing this, and his keen observations resulted in his becoming one of the richest men in America. If Wal-Mart prospers by selling what's hot, don't you think you could, too?

- Never procrastinate when rounding up hot products. If you get on the phone to reorder a product, stay on the phone until you get what you want. Waiting for call-backs or taking time out for other routine matters will kill your sales.

- The best way to capitalize on a mistake is to turn a disadvantage into an advantage. Sometimes the worst mistake you can make is to do nothing at all.

- Always keep in mind "Maximum return–minimal risk." It's not easy to accomplish, but an aggressive posture examining all outcomes may just show you an opportunity you never thought existed.

Leap Off the Cliff
A Career Change Can Be the Most Invigorating Experience of Your Life

> Always listen to experts. They'll tell you what can't be done and why. Then do it.
>
> —Robert Heinlen

For many centuries, a person's place in society was determined by his job. There was the nobility, then the merchant class, then a host of craftsmen whose skills and tools were handed down from generation to generation. Often, people were so identified with a profession that it became part of their name—e.g., John the Smith, James the Tanner, and possibly, Stu the Tailor.

The practice of naming people for their line of work stopped long ago, but until the last decade or so, almost all Americans stayed for a lifetime with the profession they chose when they entered the work force. A person was an accountant, a salesperson, a truck driver, etc. And it was more the rule than the exception for a person to stay in that line of work with one company for decades, if not an entire career.

No more. As I have discussed before in this book, the winds of change blow with such force that entire companies, entire industries, can disappear in a matter of years. If you're under thirty-five, your reward for having the same loyalty to your profession or your company as your father or grandfather did is likely to be a broken heart and broken dreams. Mid-life career changes are no longer the risky gambles of a few, but a necessary choice for the many.

After all you've read in this book, I'd be surprised if you didn't intellectually accept my argument that career changes will become a necessary routine; I'll also be surprised if the prospect doesn't terrify you. I call this principle Leap Off the Cliff, because that's the way you're going to feel. However, my job is to convince you that if you're prepared, you'll find a soft landing.

How do I know? The best evidence is the experience of millions of working women. In the last two decades, two-income families have become the rule, not the exception; two-thirds of all adult women and three-quarters of college-educated women are now in the work force. Most have had to interrupt their careers or leave good jobs because of family responsibilities or because their husbands were transferred. Most have not been able to go back to the same jobs or hop on the same career track when it's time to work again. Their only option: career change.

In some cases, women's career changes meant starting over in low-level or dead-end jobs. But in an increasing number of cases, women have decided to avoid career traps and start their own businesses. In the last five years, women have started more than two-thirds of all new businesses in the United States. In 1991 alone, women started 600,000 businesses. Others are forging alliances with companies, sharing part-time employment, working as consultants, or heading spin-off subsidiaries. Career change has been exciting, fulfilling, and financially rewarding for many of these women.

My attitude about career change evolved directly from my growing knowledge of the fad business. I began to realize that I had to start paying attention not only to what products would be hot tomorrow, but to what careers would be hot. During the last recession, at least half the companies in my industry were shrunk, crippled, or bankrupted. I saw this as my first real opportunity to pursue additional career objectives and satisfy a passion I'd had for years.

So I examined a number of fields. The first to catch my attention was sports radio. I'd always been a sports fanatic, and I was very comfortable in front of audiences and microphones. I couldn't help noticing that the one bright spot in the generally dismal financial statements of television and radio stations were the new all-sports stations. In fact, New York's WFAN, the pioneer of all-sports programming, earned more advertising revenue in 1991 than any station in the country. As a result, it was sold during that year for an incredible $70 million.

I've described elsewhere how I went about entering the sports radio business. But I have to emphasize again that the reason for my success was my confidence in my ability and my refusal to listen to the external and internal voices that said, "You're not qualified. . . . You don't have experience. . . . You're too old. . . . You're living in a dream world."

And I didn't stop at a second career. I never put all my eggs in one basket and I never stop looking around. Another great opportunity presented itself with end of the cold war, the break-up of the Soviet Union, and the eruption of democracy in eastern Europe. Like other businesspeople, I thought, "In what areas could I benefit?" Obviously, it will be a long time before the economies of the former Soviet block are healthy enough to furnish disposable incomes for imported fad items. So I thought about what those countries could export.

Reading the sports pages provided one answer: athletes trained and nurtured by the government machines that made the USSR and East Germany Olympic powerhouses. The NHL and the NBA were signing hockey and basketball players—but I didn't own a team. However, with some connections I'd made as a sports broadcaster, I *could* get into boxing. The Soviet Union and Eastern Europe were storehouses of boxing talent, and the fighters desperately wanted to move to the West to make a living.

Through my contacts I became a boxing promoter. We have a group of talented athletes in training and promising television contracts. I hope to have a world champion or two in our corner in the next two or three years.

I've also turned my attention to publishing (obviously) and motivational speaking. I've always wanted to bring my message about taking the pulse of the consumer and embracing change to a wide audience. Most recently, I decided to meet the demands for speakers and broaden our message. Once again, I asked: What other kinds of people would have something to say about changing jobs in mid-life? Another obvious answer: professional athletes, whose careers end in their thirties or, in rare cases, in their forties. Therefore, I am in the process of forming a speakers bureau, in conjunction with a number of prominent ex-athletes, to provide speaking and promotional services to a wide variety of audiences.

The variety of new careers I've explored may seem overwhelming. But I recommend everyone cultivate a similar number of options. Let me explain why. If you were (or are) a sales manager for a large company, I doubt if you'd be doing your job if you only called a handful of current customers. Instead, you probably pitch double or triple the number of prospective customers, cultivating them over time. If you don't, you won't increase your current sales; in fact, you'll be in serious trouble if you lose any current customers.

Every single one of us—from truck driver to accountant—is a sales manager for ourselves. We owe ourselves the same sales effort we could supply to our employer. That's why we all have to cultivate several different career options. Not only is this an excellent way to expand our income, it's vital protection in the case our current job or our current employer disappears.

How do you decide what other careers to explore? Give in to your daydreams. List your interests. Talk to people. Make contacts. Volunteer your services in appropriate areas. You'd be surprised how far sheer enthusiasm and energy can get you.

Finally, the most important sales job you can do is a sales job on yourself. You have to convince yourself that a "leap off the cliff" won't be fatal. Instead, it can be leaping from a dead-end position into any one of a number of far more exciting and more lucrative opportunities. The future belongs to those of us who have faith in ourselves, who despise the word *can't*, who are willing to try new things, who are willing to admit that we have to learn and don't know it all. I'm one of those people: I hope you are, too.

Some Things to Think About

- Pretend you're a kid and play "What do you want to be when you grow up?" You've probably found yourself envying people in certain kinds of jobs. So make a list. No doubt some are impractical—for example, my chances of making the NBA are now pretty slim. But making a list is a good place to start.

- Talk to people about their jobs. You may learn surprising facts that present certain careers in a new light. Ask questions, particularly about opportunities in that field. Your questions may lead to an invitation to talk further.

• Listen carefully when someone approaches you about a new job, even if it's in a field you're unfamiliar with. Sometimes, other people may have a different perspective on your abilities than you do.

Peer Into the Crystal Ball
The Dangerous But Exciting Pastime of Forecasting the Future

> How ludicrous and outlandish is astonishment at anything that may happen in life.
>
> —Marcus Aurelius

Many pages ago, at the very beginning of this book, I explained that I always make a point of explaining that my success in finding and profiting from fads had nothing to do with any psychic powers or special prognostication skills. I have also emphasized several times that the quickest way to go broke is to bet the fort on what you think will happen or hope will happen instead of on what information from the marketplace tells you is happening. On a day-to-day basis, I'm the ultimate realist.

However, that doesn't mean I don't thoroughly enjoy an occasional daydream about the future. I think it's a lot of fun to speculate about what's going to happen in the years and decades to come. I find thinking about the future to be mind expanding, making me more receptive to unusual or different ideas that my more rational self, the self that operates my business, might instantly dismiss. If the events of the last few years haven't convinced you that the most outlandish events can occur, nothing will.

I want to say again that making predictions doesn't mean you have to put any money where your mind is. I thoroughly enjoy making football predictions on my sports talk show, and I normally enjoy impressive success. But I'm also sure that my success—and my enjoyment—could vanish quickly if I started betting on those predictions.

Given those restrictions, let me share with you a few of my thoughts about the future of fads and the consumer marketplace.

• Note the new "chameleon principle." That is, good guys change into bad guys and bad guys change into good guys nearly overnight these days. Two outstanding examples: the breakup of the Soviet Union turned Russia into a good guy; George Bush went from record high approval ratings after Desert Storm to record low approval ratings a few months later.

Volatility in public opinion presents both opportunities and dangers for fad entrepreneurs. Opportunities for fad sales are always stronger when public opinion is strong on any given subject, whether it's military intervention in a remote part of the world or the victory of a sports team. But shifting public opinion also means that risking money on any long-term involvement in a product or service could produce a disaster when public opinion switches.

The way to protect yourself is to assume that public opinion and public likes and dislikes could change the next day. Keep every possible line of communication open, from contact with influential people to devouring newspapers and news reports. Feedback is your only protection.

• Young people have, in the past, almost always been the fad makers—but this is about to change. The youth audience has traditionally been the target of marketers peddling everything from clothing to fad merchandise. This audience is so desirable that as recently as 1992, NBC dumped such popular shows as "Golden Girls" and "In the Heat of the Night" because their audiences were deemed "too old" to appeal to advertisers. But in making this decision, NBC made the mistake of failing to under-stand that the demographic balance in this country is profoundly shifting. The teenage population is shrinking as the baby boomers have moved into their forties. By the year 2010, one-quarter of Americans will be age sixty-five or older. These Americans have substantial discretionary income, and they will use it on their own type of fad items. These fads will, no doubt, be much different from mood rings or Moonie dolls. But anyone who is tuned into this huge and rapidly growing market is sure to prosper.

• Over the next few years, think practical when evaluating products. I know that I defined fad products as merchandise that had little or no practical value. By that I meant fads don't satisfy any of the basic requirements of life—shelter, food, clothing, medical care, etc. However, consumers in the 1990s are holding almost every purchase up to a new set of standards. T-shirts will continue to be popular because they can be worn, not just displayed. Cabbage Patch Dolls and trolls are toys that have play value for children for weeks, even months after purchase. But consumers today seem to have a delay switch on their impulse buying that causes hesitation before making a purchase. "Is this worth the money?" flashes through minds today, in stark contrast to the attitude of the 1970s and 1980s. If you can make any sort of practical argument for your product, you'll be a step up on your competition in today's environment.

• Recognize the profound changes in the structure of retail business in the United States today. Increasingly, large areas of retailing, from party goods to office supplies, are being dominated by superstores or warehouse stores filled with massive quantities of items sold at significant, everyday discounts. Office superstores like Staples have put thousands of local stationery stores out of business. The positive side of this retailing revolution is that other small businesses, who didn't have the clout to negotiate large discounts with individual suppliers, find their cost for office supplies and services dropping significantly. One entrepreneur in the child-care business told me that she's cut her purchasing costs nearly 30 percent over the last two years. Any such cost reduction is good news for a lot of people.

However, at the same time, the sudden rise of the superstore had made marketing fad and novelty items much more difficult. Those mom-and-pop stationery stores nearly always sold such merchandise. I could always persuade some of these stores to try a new product—if it rushed out of the store, I knew I was onto something and I could quickly make a larger investment in the product. I benefited and the manufacturer benefited.

The superstores, on the other hand, carry a much more limited selection of merchandise. They generally won't touch a product unless a huge demand has already been demonstrated and unless large quantities of the merchandise are readily available. This makes it much more difficult to launch a product or a product line.

The trend toward superstores in an economic climate in which price is important will surely continue. It's profound effect on would-be fad makers or fad finders has to be taken into account.

• Explore the new marketing frontiers—cable television and
direct mail. It's impossible to turn on television late at
night or early on weekend mornings without finding an
infomercial airing. These half-hour shows, hosted by a
quasi-celebrity and packaged like a talk show, are really
long advertisements for products that range from success
systems to kitchen appliances. The reason for their popularity and success is that direct marketing to the consumer is often the best way to launch a new product or
service in an economy dominated by superstores.

Their appeal, I think, is related to the one major
drawback of warehouse clubs and superstores—they make
shopping a substantial headache. Superstores are crowded,
noisy, and offer minimal, if any, sales help. In stark
contrast, shopping from one's home by telephone is
comfortable and convenient. A large segment of the public
has purchased products marketed in this way.

Perhaps the best and most profitable example is Richard
Simmons's *Rockin' to the Oldies* series of taped exercise
programs. Simmons has made a fortune exclusively
through the use of infomercials—money he might not have
made in any other way.

You may want to dismiss cable advertising and direct
mail as too expensive for anyone without substantial capital.
However, ads on some local cable systems are priced as low
as ten dollars for sixty seconds. Understanding how such
advertising works and judicious experimenting with it may
offer the best change for small entrepreneurs to grow.

• Don't ignore the global economy. As we learned when
we watched the Persian Gulf War in our living rooms,
television has truly made the world a global village.
Every aspect of our lives, from our jobs to our culture,
is profoundly influenced by what's happening in other
areas of the world.

We hear a lot of bad news about what the Japanese, the
Germans, and other countries are doing to our economy.
Hidden in this bad news is that American exports have
been by far the strongest aspect of our economy since
1990. I believe we've only begun to tap the immense
potential that exists in so many areas of the world—not
only Europe and Asia, but in Africa and South America as
well. Perhaps the only industry that takes full advantage of
overseas markets is the movie industry—for some films,

worldwide grosses are triple the U.S. gross.

Because we Americans have been so provincial for so
many years, we forget that people in other countries buy
on impulse, too. If you remember, one of the reasons for
Batman's revival was a groundswell of interest in the old
TV series in England. I haven't been involved in major
international fads—but I wouldn't wage a nickel that I
won't be in the future. I plan to keep my eye on what's hot
in foreign countries, and I think you should, too.

- Remember America's increasingly diverse population.
Waves of immigration have been changing the face of this
land since the first explorers stepped off their sailing ships.
That's why it's astounding to me that so many people
assume that the population mix suddenly froze when the
last great European immigrations were over.

   U.S. census figures tell a different story. Over the course
of the next decade, so-called minority groups will make up
between 25 percent and 50 percent of the population.
These groups are made up of hard-working, ambitious
people who are pulling themselves up the economic ladder.
They, too, have substantial and growing discretionary
income—and the impulse to spend some of it on fad
merchandise. Again, I haven't experienced significant sales
of fad merchandise targeted specifically at minority groups.
But as with international fads, I am sure that there will be
such fads in the future. I have decided to pay increasing
attention to the success and failures of companies making
specific minority marketing efforts to see what I can learn.
When something gets hot, I'll be ready to step in.

- Pay attention to technology. I've always been a people
person, not a computer person. I spend most of my time
on the telephone, and although I appreciate the advantages
computers and fax machines have provided in supporting
our sales effort, I haven't put them center stage in my
business.

   But I can't help being totally astonished by how far
technology has come in such a short period of time.
Salespeople walk into my office carrying briefcase-sized
computers with the data processing capability of computers
that filled entire rooms little more than a decade ago.
From my office, a salesperson can use a modem to get
an inventory of supplies in distant warehouses, verify the
status of a shipment, access daily sales and returns by

region of the country, even transfer money or arrange a letter of credit.

I don't think I'll ever stop using personal contact as my primary source of information about what's happening in my field all across the country. But I have pledged to pay more attention to the growth and sophistication of computer data bases that may provide valuable detailed information that I may have overlooked. Repeatedly in this book I've emphasized how important gathering information is to making money in fads.

There's also another reason to become computer-literate. As technology dominates our economy, there are bound to be more and more electronic fads. I know that I won't be quick enough to pick up the fads or sophisticated enough to intelligently negotiate with suppliers unless I understand the technology. Again, there are fortunes to be made.

Some Things to Think About

- Reserve a little time each week for daydreaming about the future. It's not only relaxing, it expands the range of possibilities you consider for yourself and your business. Big business if often built on big dreams.

- Look for intelligently written magazine articles and books like *Megatrends 2000* that include some expert opinions on what the future will be like. Most of the authors' specific predictions will be wrong, but the evidence they marshal to support these predictions is very enlightening. They encourage you to think about what will happen tomorrow instead of brooding about what happened yesterday.

- Acquire enough knowledge about computers to follow the articles in computer magazines written for the general public, such as *PC*. I have friends who are very stubborn about admitting the importance of technology—I remind them it makes about as much sense as did refusing to watch television in the 1940s. You can't stop the future.

Index